...Y TO

50

How to Live with Gratitude, Grace, and the Effects of Gravity

LAURIE RUSSELL

elevate
faith

PUBLISHED in Boise, Idaho by Elevate Faith.
An imprint of Elevate Publishing.

THIS BOOK MAY BE PURCHASED in bulk for educational, business, organizational, or promotional use.

FOR INFORMATION, please email info@elevatepub.com

PAPERBACK ISBN-13: 9781943425310

EBOOK ISBN-13: 9781943425808

LIBRARY OF CONGRESS CONTROL NUMBER: 2016942589

PRINTED IN THE UNITED STATES OF AMERICA.

CONTENTS

INTRODUCTION

I have a vague recollection of the day my mom turned 50. Many details of that day I've already forgotten, but one thing I do remember thinking is, "Man, she's getting old!"

She didn't look 50, and she definitely didn't act it. My mom has always been active, scurrying around watching other people's kids or cutting the grass of an elderly neighbor. I'm sure all the movement kept her young at heart and in good physical shape, but the thought of her being half-a-century old was mind boggling.

Now I'm on the eve of turning 50 myself, and I have similar thoughts. Part of me still feels like a crazy 20 year old who could fearlessly run in a bathing suit, Baywatch style. But, now, when I see myself wearing one in the mirror, I'm quickly reminded that I really am almost half-a-century old.

Even if the urge to jog on the beach in a bathing suit did overcome my sensibilities, the rumbling from my thighs smashing together or the jolting of my post-baby belly would probably throw me off balance, thrust me into a face plant, and tear my ACL. (I apologize if the thought of this just made you throw up a little bit in your mouth.)

My mind battles back and forth. One part wants to set new goals and tackle exciting challenges. It doesn't want to sit on the sideline in my middle-age years. Instead, it wants to dream new dreams and see more of the world.

The other side wants to hang up the dreams and let my kids pick up where I left off. It believes it would easier for me to live vicariously through them. The thought of sitting in a lounger without the guilt of thinking "I should be doing such and such" sounds kind of nice.

But then you wonder: *Is one desire better than the other? Or, is this new phase of life a mixture of both?*

Maybe the answer is different for each of us. God did make us all unique.

However, there is a huge difference between *giving up* and *letting go.* Giving up, you quit trying. Letting go, you adjust certain ideas to meet your present reality—but you continue to move forward and get better in the process.

Giving up is easy. Letting go takes effort and can be painful—but it frees you to become anew.

Let Me Illustrate:

During the summer of 2015, I was in a funk. Our family was on vacation in Whitefish, Montana. I was up early while the rest of my family slept. I didn't want to wake them, so I sat on the balcony, with a fresh cup of coffee, taking in the beautiful scenery around me.

Sounds like a perfect morning, right?

I was miserable. I had endured another sleepless night and now faced a hopeless morning. At the time, I didn't know why. My family was healthy, our business was growing, and our children were happy. I should have been filled with hope and joy, but instead I was plagued with despair.

I had lost my purpose. My children were 12 and 14 and were more independent. Our growing company felt as if it had outgrown me, and I no longer felt drawn to work in the office. Add to that, my health had begun to concern me.

Two years ago, I was in the best shape of my life. I completed a 70.3 Ironman triathlon and had endless energy. I was at a healthy weight and a picture of good health.

But then, last summer, my blood pressure was high. I had gained 10 pounds in one year. Sleep avoided me, and stress consumed me.

Two years ago, I wrote my first book, started a speaking career, blogged regularly (well, "regularly" for someone with ADD), and helped run our publishing company.

That day, I found myself floundering. I halfway completed tasks and went to bed each night feeling guilty because I had gone postal on the kids and overwhelmed because I just wasn't getting anything done.

Prior, I was a driven person. But now I was only going through the motions. I had never been diagnosed officially, but I regularly dealt with bouts of depression and did a good job of hiding it from others. The episodes never lasted long, but they continually drained the life out of me.

As I sat on the balcony that morning, I prayed, "God, help me. I can't keep living like this. Nothing excites me. I'm passionate about nothing. Help me get through this *funk*. I feel as if I'm failing in every area of my life. Why am I here? What am I supposed to do in this next phase of my life? I want to truly laugh again."

I was stuck on the porch that morning. I couldn't watch TV because of my sleeping family. We had no Internet or cell service to distract me, so all I could do was look at God's beautiful creation and think over what I had just prayed.

What can I do to get out of this gloom? How did I get so bad off?

I thought about the most important areas of my life: my *family*, my *faith*, my *health*, and having *fun*. At this point I felt the nudge.

Focus on each of these areas, and start by taking one step in each to change your circumstances. Then write about it.

This gave me hope. Hope that change was coming. It was something that I could be passionate about, and I believed it could help me become whole again.

A week later, three women separately shared with me similar struggles. I wasn't alone. I knew then that my journey was supposed to be something that I shared—the good, the bad, and the funny. It gave me back a purpose, and it felt as if God was telling me not to give up (so often, this seemed a reasonable choice), but instead, to let go of preconceived notions.

Getting still and alone with God that morning, free from electronic distractions, I was able to examine the true condition of my heart and cry out to God. It was there He handed me a rope, or maybe it was a string, but it was enough to give me the hope I needed to move from giving up to letting go.

Letting go of the lie that I am no longer of worth to others.

Letting go of the belief that I need to be all things to all people.

Letting go of the desire to look like a 20 year old in my middle age.

Letting go of the fear of failure.

Letting go of perfection.

I've found that letting go is very freeing. There's less baggage to weigh you down.

This book shares practical tips and lessons I learned in my personal journey to regain a holistic lifestyle in areas of family, health, faith, and fun. My desire is that it will be a helpful resource and encouragement to you in your own journey into middle age.

I've broken the material up into small sections to make it easy to read in quick five- to 15-minute sessions. (Five if I have my readers, 15 if I can't find them.) If you're like me, my best time for reading is at night. However, I'm usually in bed about 15 minutes before my hormone pill begins to kick in, and God knows I'm going to choose sleep over reading, even though I love reading. If you struggle with the same battle, I wrote this book with you in mind. Why can't we live in a world where sleep and reading can coexist?!

So, let's work through this aging thing together. It should not be something we dread, but something we celebrate and embrace. A time of gaining and sharing wisdom and cheering each other on—toasting to our victories and laughing at our mistakes.

We may be scared we'll fall flat on our face. But that's far better than shriveling up and dying, which is guaranteed to happen if we choose to give up.

Grab my hand, my friend. Let's dump those things that weigh us down and venture onto this road together.

SECTION
1

OVERWHELMED NO MORE

> ### "IF YOU DON'T KNOW WHERE YOU ARE GOING, YOU MIGHT WIND UP SOMEPLACE ELSE."
> ### —YOGI BERRA

Is it just me, or am I the only one out there who is in a constant state of feeling overwhelmed?

I'm constantly moving from one activity to another, but never fully experiencing where I am presently because, in my mind (which is already working on a deficit), I'm planning out how to make it to my next appointment, buy supplies for the school project, send the text to confirm carpool, plan out dinner, and leave a note reminding my son to pick up the dog poop before the garbage is picked up.

All of it is good stuff, well, minus the dog poop, but that's my real life. Looking over the "to-do" lists that constantly flood my brain, I find there is no way around these tasks. But they have this sneaky way of stealing my focus so I'm never fully present anywhere, and I'm walking around in circles, rarely moving forward.

Isn't one of the fringe benefits of getting older that we're no longer in a phase of being in a constant state of stress? Your kids are older. Your career is established. You own your weekends once more. I don't know about your life, but mine looks nothing like this, and I'm beginning to feel like I've been robbed of the "good life" in this aging business.

Then I look in the mirror, and it glares back at me the reality of the number of years I have lived. A family of ants could hide in some of the lines on my face. And don't get me started on my backside. There is a reason God didn't give us eyes on the back of our heads. If I had to look at that thing rumble all day as I walked, I'd never get out of bed.

I know 50 is still young, but a new decade does put a sense of urgency in you. Time is flying by even faster now, and the busyness around me often robs me of fully enjoying each moment. It's not just about moving forward, but also being fully present.

I've had many conversations with friends and family who have this same struggle, so I know I'm not alone. Many of us are dealing with the same sense of feeling overwhelmed, but not clearly knowing the source.

If we're not careful, our circumstances will steal our attention and have us walking all over the map with no final destination in mind. Before we know it, we're stressed-out zombies marching around everywhere, unfulfilled.

That's not living. It's time to make a few minor adjustments to take back our lives.

CHAPTER 1
REDEFINING AGING

"IF YOU DON'T LIKE SOMETHING, CHANGE IT. IF YOU CAN'T CHANGE IT, CHANGE YOUR ATTITUDE."
—MAYA ANGELOU

Why does our culture look at aging as a death sentence? Okay—bad choice of words. But why is it something that we dread?

When we are younger we can't wait to be older, but when we're older we spend endless hours, and large sums of money, to look and feel younger.

I get the frustration of dealing with body aches. The challenge of finding reading glasses to buy that look cute on you (and then finding them when you need them)! Or seeing a photo of you posted on the Internet (which is there *forever*) while you were running in the local 5K and all you see is the crepey skin on your thighs that looks like, well…multiple folds of crepe paper!

Believe me, I know it's not always fun. But those of us with some ~~decades~~ years on us do have a lot to bring to the table (and I'm not talking about extra fiber).

I know there are times we don't see it because we're too focused looking into the mirror at what we're losing instead of building upon all that we have gained over the years. And, let's give it to ourselves, we have a lot to give. (We may just forget about it sometimes due to our over-stuffed brains.)

There's a lot of awesomeness in each and every one of us.

No, really. The awesomeness is there. But our culture has trained our eyes to first see the thunder thighs crossing the finish line instead of celebrating the fact that we just ran a 5K, or a 10K, or a marathon in our 40s, 50s, 60s, and more. We may not be able to walk down the stairs afterwards, but we should be celebrating the inner strength within us and wear that medal with pride.

We live in a time when it's not unheard of to go back to school in your 40s, to start a new career in your 50s, to run longer in your 60s, and travel farther and fully live life in your 70s. We don't have to give up and just accept our present circumstances. We can make the changes to find and live the life that we've always longed for.

Our world is changing. We're working longer. We're living longer. But, if we don't redefine what it means to age, we'll give up earlier. We'll stop living sooner because we're allowing an old-school mentality to limit our possibilities. Forty is not too old to adopt a baby. Fifty is not too old to run in your first 5K road race. Sixty is not too old to take your first overseas trip. Seventy is not too old to remarry.

We may need to make some adjustments along the way. That's okay. Sometimes, it's more fun not knowing how things will turn out. It keeps life more interesting. At the same time, making adjustments doesn't equal throwing in the towel. We may require more rest or extra effort, but that doesn't negate the value of our accomplishments.

Our generation is doing more than previous ones ever thought possible, and we're modeling to the next generations that *everything* is possible. We only need to convince our minds, trust our hearts, and push our bodies.

It's time we begin to redefine what it means to age. If we're still breathing, we should still be living.

"THE HARDEST THING IN LIFE TO LEARN IS WHICH BRIDGE TO CROSS AND WHICH TO BURN."
—DAVID RUSSELL

DON'T LET WHAT OTHERS **THINK** DICTATE YOUR **PURPOSE.**

When people ask me about the topic of my website and I tell them it's my journey to turning 50, many of them look embarrassed for me, as if I just told them I had beans for lunch, and now I'm dealing with flatulence. (Now that I think about it, maybe that is what they think I'm writing about!) I guess talking about getting older is not the coolest topic.

If I'm not careful, I let their response get in my head, and I begin to doubt if what I'm doing is helping anyone or if it is just a silly project to occupy my time. Immediately, I'm tempted to quit and continue living my safe and secure life.

Most of these responses came from people much younger, and I had to remind myself, they don't understand the struggles yet. One of the benefits of being older is that you don't care as much about what other people think. (Of course, that could be due to forgetting about it before it gets into your head.)

However, the middle-school-style judging is still there. The only difference is the taunting this time doesn't always come from another. Instead, it often comes from the voices inside our own head, telling you you're foolish even to think you're capable of accomplishing your dream. Some of these voices may be from people in your past. Or they may solely be your own voice.

Only way to silence them is to step out of the box that has been holding you hostage, and move far enough away from it so that you can no longer hear them. You may feel exposed as you step out of your comfort zone. This is natural. Most of us don't particularly enjoy the feeling of standing naked before our family and friends. But we can't let the fear of failure keep us in our comfort zone. It's all part of the process, and we have to use each failure as a stepping stone, bringing us closer to our goal.

When we are fulfilling our purpose, we're different. We're vibrant. We're positive. We're energetic. We're risk-takers. When we're hiding in our comfort zones, we go through the motions. We're bored, and our life loses meaning. We must tune out the negative voices in our heads and, instead, listen to ones cheering us on and believe that we've been given everything we need to accomplish our goals, realizing that age is not an excuse to slow us down. By doing so, we not only set the bar higher for ourselves, we show younger generations that age is not something to be feared. It's not a negative. It's a beautiful time in life where we not only have the talent and ability, but that they are wrapped tightly with the wisdom we've learned along the way.

Don't let the opinions of others stall you. Go for it!

"WRINKLES SHOULD MERELY INDICATE WHERE SMILES HAVE BEEN."
—MARK TWAIN

WHAT BEAUTY MEANS TO YOU.

Years ago, I shared this story on my blog. One morning I was working from home and knew that I was not going to see anyone until late afternoon. The kids were at school, my husband, Mark, was at the office, so, to save time, this city girl went with the "natural" look. No makeup. Just me, my computer, and a comfy pair of sweats. I fixed a cup of tea and began working.

About an hour later, the doorbell rang. I peeked out the window and saw it was our delivery guy in search of a signature. When I opened the door, he looked at me and seemed thrown off a bit, "Oh, you're home. I sure hope I didn't wake you." Huh? Why did he say that? I didn't delay in answering the door. It was almost 10:00 a.m. on a weekday. Why would he think I'd still be in bed?

As I returned to my desk, I glanced at my reflection in the mirror. I stopped. I knew. My face, normally covered with beauty products, was completely bare. My imperfections glared. My eyes seemed smaller, my nose looked bigger, and my hair was definitely nappier. I looked more like a woman fresh out of bed, rather than one fresh for the day.

The rest of the morning was spent with me obsessing over my lack of "natural" beauty. I have a love/hate relationship with beauty. The old saying tells us that "beauty is in the eyes of the beholder," but, if this is true, why do I feel enslaved to it? Why do I feel the need for my body to be a certain size and my hair to be a certain color (or rather *not* a certain color, ahem, gray)? Why is it that I can find beauty on the TV, but not in the mirror?

Perhaps part of the problem is our culture's misconstrued definition of beauty. Dictionaries define beauty as something that brings great pleasure to the senses or blesses the mind. I like this. According to this definition, beauty can be found basically anywhere.

I did an informal word search in a Bible program on the words "beauty" and "beautiful" and noticed two things. First, with the exception of the books of Esther and Song of Solomon, these two words were generally used to describe God or part of His creation. The second usage of these words warned us of the dangers of depending on our own man-made creation. Again, this was an informal word study, but it appears that God knew that our obsession for beauty would take our eyes off of Him and what He has given us, and then place it on ourselves.

We like beauty. We want it and will do what it takes to have it. (Most of the time. There are some areas I will never wax!) I personally don't see harm in trying to improve my appearance, but when it becomes my focus, it puts me in "insecurity" territory. I see all that I'm not, or not anymore. It's a balance. I have to look beyond the mirror. The mirror will lie to us by pointing out *physical* imperfections.

We have to look and see the beauty *within* us. This is the beauty that causes our smiles to reach our eyes. This is the beauty that sees a friend in need and reaches out to help them. This is the beauty that doesn't fade with time. This is the beauty that loves unconditionally (or at least tries). This is the beauty that helps others succeed. This is the beauty that will cry with a friend. This is the beauty that will celebrate with a foe. This is the beauty that will help heal and unify a world that is crumbling at the seams. This is the beauty that sees no color. It is a beauty that only sees love.

This is the beauty that is within us all. We just need to focus on it.

For now, I'll continue to wear makeup most days, and I may never see my natural hair color again. Come to think of it, I'm not sure if I remember what that color actually is. Either way, when the gray makes its way through every six to seven weeks, I'm working to retrain my brain to see it as a reminder that God has given me some great years and memories, and hopefully some wisdom along the way.

Our greatest beauty is from within. Nothing can ever take that away from us.

Aging does not mean life is over. It's a new door to a new phase of life with another adventure attached to it. The only way we experience it is if we open the door and run through it.

Consider This:

- Rewrite the definition of age. What do you see in your future?

- Looking in the mirror reveals flaws. Looking in your soul reveals dreams. What dreams do you see?

- The voices in your head don't want to see you thrive. Don't engage them. Be their boss and fire those suckers.

CHAPTER 2

GET GOING

"IF AND WHEN WERE PLANTED AND NOTHING GREW."
—PROVERB

I knew I needed change.

That summer morning on the porch was a wake-up call. I knew I needed to work on many areas of my life. It was fun to talk and dream about how I'd do it, but getting started was a whole other project.

I had an excuse for everything. An issue with our insurance allowed me to postpone going to the doctor. And, because I didn't have doctor's clearance, I really shouldn't do much exercising. The snowy weather kept me from having photos made for the website. Without photos, it was too soon to hire a web designer. I didn't want to write the content until I had finalized the web design.

Yada yada yada.

It doesn't take long to see I have an issue with procrastination. I tried it with giving birth, but that didn't work out too well for me.

However, this time it felt different. Something stronger was keeping me from moving forward with this project. I tried to be all spiritual about it and say maybe it was God who wanted me to hold off? Mark quickly reminded me that if I waited too long, it would be hard to have a blog on my journey to 50. Especially if I was in my 60s.

Party pooper.

It wasn't until I heard an interview with Steven Pressfield, author of the book *The War of Art*. He said we were all created with a *genius* within us, a calling, a purpose for our lives. But there is an enemy of creativity that he calls the Resistance. He went on to say, "If you believe in God (and I do), then the Resistance would be evil trying to prevent us from achieving the life God intended for us."

Hello.

This gave me the motivation to get up and start working. In a weird way, it gave more purpose to my project. If I didn't do it, I'd miss the opportunity to encourage others and possibly help someone else in need.

We are all unique in our gifts and talents. If we use them correctly, they are a threat to the enemy who doesn't want to see us become all that God created in us.

There is a cocktail of wisdom, knowledge, talent, strength, insight, etc. inside of you that no one else can replicate. It's divinely made for you and your circumstances. If you don't take that first step, no one will see it, including you.

IF YOU KNOW WHAT'S HOLDING YOU DOWN, YOU STOP MAKING EXCUSES AND STAND UP TO FIGHT IT.

Don't avoid pain. There is purpose and a lot of beauty discovered and created while in the midst of pain. Many of the great artists among us are great because they didn't try to remove the pain in their lives. Instead, they dug deep in order to understand and conquer it. They worked through it, and it was there they found their inspiration for their art. They painted the great portrait. They composed a beautiful melody. They choreographed that famous ballet. They etched the words that healed souls.

Pain doesn't feel good, and it's natural for us to want to avoid it as a survival technique. But not all pain destroys. Much like an athlete who endures the stress of a hard workout, their muscles ache, begging them to stop, but those who don't quit become stronger. Pain can reveal to us greatness that is hidden, dormant for years inside of us that has been covered by comfort. By enduring and conquering pain, we can *all* learn to create and understand on levels we never knew possible.

Don't excuse away pain. Don't avoid pain.

Face it head on. Work through it, and allow it to peel away layers that are masking the true greatness within you. It's there. You just need to start cutting away at it.

"LIFE WAS MEANT TO BE LIVED, AND CURIOSITY MUST BE KEPT ALIVE. ONE MUST NEVER, FOR WHATEVER REASON, TURN HIS BACK ON LIFE."
—ELEANOR ROOSEVELT

MOVING FORWARD IS HARD WORK, AND THE FIRST STEP IS THE HARDEST.

One day, Mark convinced me to go on an easy run with him. I had by now been to the doctor and was given medical clearance to exercise. However, my crazy schedule made it hard to do anything consistently, so I was still out of shape.

We were about a half mile in, and I went all whiny on him, "This is hard. I don't feel good. I think I want to turn around now."

"No, keep going. You know what they say, the hardest part is the first mile. After that it will get easier, once your body is warmed up."

What did he know? He wasn't sucking for air like I was. I was tempted to trip him, but we were in front of our pastor's condo. Knowing my luck, he would just happen to look out his window as I used my foot to knock Mark's legs out from under him. So I decided to be the bigger person and let it go. (Isn't Mark lucky to have me as his wife?)

So, instead, I had to tough it out and, of course, he was right. My breathing fell into a rhythm, the pain in my legs eventually went numb, and even though I never felt great *during* the run, I did feel great afterwards and was glad I didn't give up.

Any change we make in our life takes effort. It's hardest in the beginning, and then, when it gets easier, you move up to the next level. It gets hard again before it gets easier—but, to me, nothing is as hard as that first step.

If you can conquer the start, you can work up to anything.

WE SHOULD
STRIVE FOR
EXCELLENCE
INSTEAD OF
PERFECTIONISM.
PERFECTIONISM
CAN PARALYZE
US.

When my kids were young, Mark's work required him to do a lot of international travel that would take him away for two weeks at a time. Of course, that meant there were times he missed certain holidays.

This particular trip, he missed Mother's Day. Noah and Anastasia, who were five and seven at the time, didn't want me to miss out, so they devised a plan. That morning, the kids snuck into my room and, in a loud whisper, (so as to not fully wake me up), they told me to stay in bed, and they'd bring me breakfast. Anastasia knew how to make muffins, and Noah knew how to make eggs.

Thirty minutes later Noah brought me tepid coffee with grounds floating on top.

An hour later they carried in a tray with overcooked eggs and blueberry muffins. I took a bite of a muffin and my mouth was filled with a strong bitter taste.

I played it off well and the mistake went unnoticed until Noah took a bite of his muffin. He gagged and spit it out onto his plate and viciously wiped his tongue with his napkin. Confused, Anastasia took a bite and ran to the sink to rinse her mouth, "What is wrong?!"

We talked over the recipe, and it turned out she had used baking soda instead of baking powder. She began crying, "I wanted it to be perfect for you so you wouldn't be lonely with Daddy gone!"

Her words melted my heart, but what she didn't realize at the time, she and Noah had given me the perfect Mother's Day because they had given me their *best* out of the purity of their hearts.

Perfection can be a curse. It hoards anxiety over us and holds us in a standstill for fear that we won't be good enough. When in reality most people want to be with us and to know we are giving our best. And, if our best isn't good enough, then perhaps *they* are not best for us.

Perfectionism kills our curiosity. We're afraid to ask, "What if?" for fear of being wrong. Progress comes from people making mistakes and learning from them. I'm on an airplane as I type this. If the Wright brothers had given up after their first failure, there's a chance that I would be typing this while riding in a car, and I can't type while riding in a car. I get carsick. Plus, I know I'm not the only one out there who learned from their mistakes by dating the wrong person.

"ONLY THOSE WHO WILL RISK GOING TOO FAR CAN POSSIBLY FIND OUT HOW FAR ONE CAN GO."
—T. S. ELIOT

Years ago, Boise hosted the 70.3 Ironman. The participants swim 1.2 miles, bike 56 miles, and then run 13.1 miles. The bike portion went along our neighborhood, so we all went to watch it. As the athletes rode by, I was in awe. They were so strong and brave. There were all body types and most of them looked like normal people, too!

We hurried to the finish and waited for them to complete the run portion. It was emotional watching the finish. They were exhausted, but elated. I had the ugly cry face going on. I couldn't believe they had all raced 70.3 miles. They were my heroes!

There was no way I could ever do anything like that.

Years later, my friend called me on the phone and convinced me to sign up.

I trained with friends over the next year, and it was a blast. However, my training was interrupted numerous times due to work, all kinds of crazy health issues ranging from a broken toe to a ruptured ovarian cyst, all of it keeping me out of training for weeks.

The morning of the race I woke up feeling like I was going to the guillotine. What was I thinking?

"I don't think I'm ready to go this distance," I told Mark. My longest bike ride, to that point, had only been 42 miles. I would have to ride 12 more than that AND swim 1.2 miles and run a half marathon, all in one day. It felt impossible. I didn't want to fail, especially in front of my family and friends.

"You are stronger than you realize. You trained enough to go this distance. You just have to believe you can," he assured me.

All along the course, friends and family waited to cheer me on. It was a hard day, the temperature was in the 90s with wind gusts of 20-30 mph. It was a long day. I wasn't fast, but I did it. Crossing the finish line was a rush of emotions. I was giddy, in disbelief. I wanted to dance and cry at the same time. Actually, I kind of did both.

I didn't know I had the ability to go that far. Never before did I believe I was strong enough. I always felt it was something only others could do. Not me.

You, my friend, are strong enough to do whatever is dreaming inside your heart. You can learn that music, you can write that book, you can climb that mountain, you can complete that degree. You just have to believe it, and take the risk. Don't let the fear of failure or the plague of perfectionism keep you in a stalemate. Begin believing it in your mind, and take that leap of faith. Get going.

FEAR OF SUCCEEDING.

One of my favorite shows over the years was *Biggest Loser*. I know there has been some hype about it recently, but even in spite of it, the contestants on that show inspire me. They have a work ethic and strength that goes beyond anything I've ever imagined possible. I can guarantee you will NEVER see me workout to the point of puking. Remember, I get whiny when it starts to hurt.

In one of the first years of the show, Jillian Michaels was talking with one of the contestants. In her "come to Jesus" moment with him, she pointed out the many times in his life he "almost made it." However, each time, right before he made it, he somehow shot himself in the foot— appearing almost as if he did so intentionally.

Could it be it's hard for us to take that first step because, deep down, we're afraid of succeeding? Success costs us. You may lose a lot of your free time, as others will demand more of you. If you succeed, people may expect more out of you, wanting you to fix their problem, create a new portrait, write the next book, act in the next play. If you succeed, others might put a target on your back. Jealousy can be brutal, and, for some reason, people like to see the successful fall from the top. If we succeed, it will hurt more if/*when* we fail. We will fail. But, after a time of success, more eyes are on you so your failures may be more public. There are magazines out there whose whole purpose is to document the failure of some wonderful people. It's really sick. But clearly we love to read about it, or the magazines wouldn't be selling millions of copies each month.

Sometimes success does bring these things, but remember, there is another side to the success.

If our motives are pure and we keep what is important to us as No. 1, we have nothing to worry about. Instead, we will propel our loved ones into a wonderful journey and will be a blessing to others along the way.

Don't be afraid to succeed. Yes, it will require more work. We need you.

"THE SOONER I FALL BEHIND, THE LONGER I HAVE TO CATCH UP."
—UNKNOWN

"TOMORROW IS OFTEN THE BUSIEST DAY OF THE WEEK."
—SPANISH PROVERB

Consider This:

- Resistance is not always clearly seen. It's clever. It can be hidden in a hobby, a relationship, a substance. Are there areas in your life you feel a struggle between two worlds that are preventing you from moving?

- Expectations are often the precursor to perfectionism. You look forward to the perfect Valentine's Day only to be disappointed when your husband buys you chocolate, forgetting you're trying to lose 10 pounds. (I'm not speaking from experience, of course.) The key is being able to decipher their best in the midst of your disappointment.

CHAPTER 3
URGENT VERSUS IMPORTANT

"WHAT IS IMPORTANT IS SELDOM URGENT, AND WHAT IS
URGENT IS SELDOM IMPORTANT."
—DWIGHT D. EISENHOWER

I love this quote by Eisenhower, but deciphering what is important from what is urgent is not always that easy. The problem we have today is that there are too many options, great options that are hard to say no to.

We all have our non-negotiables, whether we would use that terminology or not. "Hi, this is my husband, Mark, and our two children, Noah and Anastasia. They are my non-negotiables."

Non-negotiables are our family and the main people in our lives, our belief systems—the filters through which everything else must go.

Beyond that, there are a lot of great things out there that I'd love to be a part of. Add in my ADD (did you see how I just used the word add and ADD in the same sentence?!), it's hard not to get distracted by wanting to be a part of everything.

I mean, I want to plant trees. I want to work toward world peace. I want to work to end child slavery. I want to take care of orphans and widows. I want to travel the world. I want to push my body beyond its limits. (Sort of. I just don't want to puke!) I want to clean the ocean. I want to build homes for the homeless.

But, to be honest, I'm pooped.

Greg McKeown, in his book, *Essentialism,* tells us that each day we are faced with a lot of trivial and a few vitals. It comes down to us choosing between the "many trivial versus the vital few." He further says that it's not about "getting more things done; it's about how to get the *right* things done."

This is a decision each of us needs to make. AND…we need to stop judging others when they make a decision we don't agree with. So, Suzie doesn't want to serve on your committee because she is homeschooling her kids.

That's okay.

And don't judge Mary, who can't cook brownies for the PTA fundraiser because she needs to prepare all night for her board meeting.

What is vital for one may be trivial for another.

The important thing is that we truly define them in our own personal lives and don't allow others—friends, bosses, colleagues, organizations, etc.—define them for us. That is between you, your family, and God.

WHAT IS
IMPORTANT
NOW WILL BE
DICTATED BY
THE PHASES
OF LIFE.

When our kids were younger, Mark and I trained for triathlons with a group of friends. It was so fun, and it worked well because our kids were at the age where they were interested in what Mom and Dad were interested in. It was a beautiful time.

Over the years, they lost interest in triathlons and wanted to endeavor into their own pursuits. For Noah it was rock climbing, track, and drums. For Anastasia, it was swimming and cello. Of course, their practice times conflicted, and the locations were on opposite sides of town. So, Mark and I now tag team to get the kids to their different practices. The only guideline we have—only one sport a season. We'll support them, but we won't go insane.

At times I wondered if we drank the Kool-Aid. When the kids were younger we swore we'd never be the parents who sold their soul to the club. We'd never sacrifice a weekend for a sport. But here we were, doing all of the above.

We have some friends who have kids a few years older than our own. The first time we got together, they told us, "We're not good friends. Right now, most of our free time is with our kids and their activities. We only have them for a few more years, and then they're gone."

We're far from being tiger parents, in fact, if we err on anything, it's probably being a little too carefree. But I love being around my kids. I love watching them play their sports and instruments. I'm blessed that they have chosen sports that attract nice kids and where I really like the other parents. These parents have become my good friends, which makes swim and track meets all the more fun.

In a few years, my children will be gone, but I believe the years we're spending together now are building a foundation for the future. Our best talks are in the car. I get to see them interact with their friends. I see and know the dynamics and can coach them on how to be better friends.

My parents did the same for me growing up, and I remember those years fondly.

I know there are single moms and parents out there who work outside the home. You don't have the freedom to drive kids to practice, much less let them be on teams. No matter. There are always opportunities to make moments we can treasure.

But my point is this—time with our loved ones is fleeting. It may be an elderly parent, it may be a colicky baby, it may be a rebellious teenager. Don't wish these moments away. Don't pray to have the trials removed from you. Instead, ask God to reveal Himself to you in them. For in these moments, a bond is built between you and your loved one.

See the joy. Make the memory. Build up the child. Give love back to the parent. Serve with the expectation of nothing in return.

Before you know it, this phase will be gone, and you will crave it—much like how I miss the days my kids ran into my arms whenever I returned home.

See the joy in the moment.

KNOW THE DIFFERENCE IN HOW MUCH IS TOO MUCH.

Did you know, when the word "priority" entered the English language in the 1400s, it was singular? The definition was the "first or prior thing." Greg McKeown points out that it remained this way until the early 1900s. It was then that we pluralized it, believing we could have "multiple first things."

But doesn't this de-prioritize things (is that a word)? It's kind of like going out on a date with your spouse, who tells you that time with you is so important, but they need to get the email out so they can focus on you...in a few minutes.

I've always said multitasking was a myth. I could never do it, and it made me feel lesser of a woman because, supposedly, it was an innate trait that all women had. I read the other day that Arianna Huffington says the same, and that it's now called "task switching." So I feel slightly redeemed.

Just because your neighbor or colleague can juggle a lot of balls, don't feel you have to add more to your handful, unless you have the extra hand (pun intended). Otherwise, you risk dropping everything, and do you really want to drop your "priorities" on their heads?

Life is not about quantity. It's about quality.

HONEY, I NEED TO BUY NEW DISHES!

At my last yearly check up with my doctor, I was informed I had gained 10 pounds. Okay, this was not new intel for me, but I was hoping my doctor also had hormone brain and would miss this small detail. There was a chance she might had it not been coupled with an increase in blood pressure.

I tried to jokingly pass it off as *white coat syndrome*, "I always get nervous when I see your doctor's white coat and *bang!* Up go my numbers."

She didn't buy it and began questioning me about my lifestyle habits. She said I was doing okay, encouraged me to get away from the computer and move more regularly, and then summed it up with, "As we age, our metabolism slows down. The best way to fight this is to cut down your portion size."

This sounded doable. I've always been somewhat of a healthy eater. I do have my vices, but I didn't need to cut them out, just cut down the size. (And, maybe how often...dang it.)

A few days later, I was proud of myself as I ate a quarter of a pizza (instead of a half of it), loaded with veggies (instead of pepperoni). For some reason I had grabbed a salad plate instead of a dinner plate and was reminded of our move to Germany several years ago. We were advised not to bring dishes with us because the American-sized dishes were often too large to fit into the smaller European cabinets. Unless we were willing to pay for custom-made cabinetry, it would be best to buy the smaller European dishes.

Maybe part of the problem is not so much our portion sizes, but rather it's the size of our plates, figuratively speaking. There's a life principle here. How many times have I complained, "I just have too much on my plate"?

Don't get me wrong. I'm not saying dream smaller or try to achieve less.

Perhaps if we had smaller plates, it would force us to truly prioritize. To truly search our hearts and figure out what it is we really want—much the same way when Mark tells me we don't have time to check luggage at the airport, that I'll need to pack everything in a carry on. Hello! Do you see the nappy hair on my head? Does he not realize how much hair product it takes to defrizz it? It's not cheap either. If TSA confiscates it, we're losing a small portion of our kids' college fund.

Don't grab for the bigger plate, one that is quickly filled with quantity. Instead, grab the smaller plate where you have to be more selective, and choose what is important.

Consider This:

- Take a look at your daily or weekly schedule. What is getting the bulk of your attention? Is it the urgent or the important things in your life?

- What are your priorities? Is there a long list battling for number one? Take some time to write them down and properly number them. Identify which is your number one and truly make it number one.

SECTION
2

OPEN RELATIONSHIPS (IT'S NOT WHAT YOU THINK)

"TO GET THE FULL VALUE OF JOY, YOU MUST HAVE SOMEONE TO DIVIDE IT WITH."
—MARK TWAIN

There are times in life you want to travel solo. It's easier. You don't have to battle with another on what to eat or where to go. There's no need to put on makeup or even shower. It's just you and the path before you, and you can stop for a potty break anytime you like without any backlash from the crew in the backseat.

I find, though, that most journeys are best when shared with others. There's more conversation, more laughter, more memories (and other minds to help recall those memories when you forget them).

However, anytime there are people living life together, there will be friction. It's not all, "Here, let me get you a piece of cake." It's more like, "Don't eat it all! I haven't had a piece yet!"

Human nature's tendency is to look at everything through the filter of "me."

How will this affect me? What will this cost me? What will this require of me?

Journeys with family may not always be a bed of roses. There are lots of thorns hidden under the leaves. But it can be oh so beautiful if we open our minds, our hearts, and our eyes to the needs of the other.

Relationships require two people. Any time there is more than one person, the odds of all parties seeing eye to eye, all the time, is next to nil. You're more likely to be struck by lightning than to have perfect harmony in your marriage. But change requires action, and action begins with a change in our thinking—a decision that we are going to do our part to improve the situation. The other party may not be on board, but if we do everything on our part to make it better, we begin to move in the right direction.

CHAPTER 4
SPOUSE: DON'T JUST LISTEN. HEAR.

"BEFORE YOU MARRY A PERSON, YOU SHOULD FIRST MAKE THEM USE A COMPUTER WITH SLOW INTERNET SERVICE TO SEE WHO THEY REALLY ARE."
—WILL FERRELL

Marriage is a bit like traveling with your spouse for a long period of time—*internationally*. It will bring about the best of you—and it will reveal the worst in you. At first, during the honeymoon period of the marriage/trip, it's perfect. Your spouse is perfect. Who cares about jetlag? You don't need sleep. You will travel anywhere, eat anything. You are in love and have each other. That is all you need.

Until weeks later, you're craving chicken nuggets for dinner, but the only thing you can find on the restaurant menu is pickled chicken feet. Your face turns blue as you hiss, "I want to go home!" All while your husband is wondering where the adventurous woman he married went.

She's still there, she's just worn down and will probably return once he's able to get you some food that will stay down. Hopefully you'll laugh about it later. But, in the meantime, the craziness of life has worn you down and is exposing an area of weakness.

Don't let me get hungry!

I really do get *hangry,* and there were moments early in our marriage where I saw pure fear in Mark's eyes, as if he were deciding whether to call 911 or a priest to perform an exorcism. I was able to articulate clearly enough, "I need food!" After I ate and he saw the personality change, he called to cancel the scheduled exorcism.

Okay, I'm exaggerating, but the point is we all have weaknesses and flaws we bring to the table. The key is to not only know this about the other, but also about yourself. Some things we need to work on, others are just part of our body's chemistry. (I really can't go long without food.) But the more we know of each other and ourselves, the more prepared we can be to keep peace on the journey.

"GROW OLD WITH ME! THE BEST IS YET TO BE."
—ROBERT BROWNING

GROW OLD TOGETHER, TRY NEW THINGS.

I grew up a city girl. The only time we ever went camping was when I was in Girl Scouts, and every time we went— no lie—it either rained or was bone-chilling cold. My troop leader wouldn't let me leave the breakfast table unless I drank my whole 8-ounce cup of grapefruit juice. I nearly puked and can't eat grapefruit today. (I'm trying not to dry heave as I'm reliving it.)

All this to say, I was not a camping fan.

However, shortly after we got married, Mark and I went on a three-week backpacking trip in…Alaska…in the backcountry…with no bathrooms…as newlyweds…with his family. It's amazing what you'll do as a newlywed. The trip was awesome, and I learned a lot of new things. (Trust me, you need to wash your hands well after using DEET.)

I figured if I could survive that trip and still love everyone in my family, I could do anything.

He convinced me to go on another three-week long camping trip…in Chile…while seven-and-a-half months pregnant…a quarter mile away from the bathroom. (Did he forget pregnant women have to get up a lot in the middle of the night to pee?!)

As we're setting up camp I hear an, "Uh oh!" from within the tent. Yep, we had forgotten to pack the sleeping bags. Did I mention it dropped down to the 40s Fahrenheit at night? It was too late to buy anything that night, so we "slept" under two towels.

I learned a lot of new things on that trip as well. Like a quarter of a mile is too far for a pregnant woman to walk by herself in the middle of the night to pee. Squatting by a tree is preemptive in helping you get your pre-pregnancy body back faster.

To be honest, I'm still not a huge camper, but I will go in an instant with my family because in the midst of these adventures, we've bonded. I love retelling these stories and, from afar, camping sounds fun. It is fun. Mark had to teach me a lot along the way.

We had to be patient with each other and try our best to model how to have a healthy "discussion" in front of our kids when Mom is tired, but there have been bears in the campsite each night, a forest fire is nearby, and she thinks it may be time to go home.

Yes, I was the one who had to learn with camping, but Mark saw the effort I made to be with him and to partake in an activity that fuels his soul. When you're open to trying new things to please the other, you make yourself vulnerable and dependent on one another, in a healthy way. Things don't get old and you can expand your repertoire of expertise. Like how to camp while nearly eight months pregnant!

"NEVER LOVE ANYONE WHO TREATS YOU LIKE YOU'RE ORDINARY."
—OSCAR WILDE

A COUPLE THAT PLAYS TOGETHER, STAYS TOGETHER.

Mark and I have been married 17 years. Like every couple, over the years, we've had our ups and downs in our relationship. But we've had a wonderful ride together, mainly because we have the same belief system, and we were friends before we began dating. We both longed to travel. We both enjoyed running and being outdoors.

Looking back over the years, the times we were the closest were either when we were in a time of crisis, with either our family or our company, or when we were playing together.

No one wants to be in a crisis long term, our bodies and minds can't handle it. But making an effort to play together is doable.

As I mentioned in the intro, recently there was a two-year period where I struggled with my health and wasn't able to do much physical activity. Our marriage was fine during this time, but something was missing.

Hindsight revealed that, unless we were on vacation, Mark and I had little play time together. We were basically coexisting and doing life. Our favorite way to spend time together is on a bike ride or run. The good endorphins are pumping. It's just the two of us, and we're able to have uninterrupted conversation. (Unless he's going too slow, and I leave him eating my dust.)

Unfortunately, my recent health issues took the joy out of exercising with Mark.

Now that I'm feeling better, we're able to bike and run together again, but it did reveal a potential issue. We may not always have our health and must therefore find other activities that we enjoy together.

It's important to find an activity that is "play" for you both. It could be going to a concert, or a movie, or reading in a coffee shop. Something that restores your soul and replenishes you both.

Be open to trying new activities. If he likes going to car races, give it a chance. Ask him about the drivers, learn about it. By making the effort, perhaps he'll be more open to entertaining your interests as well.

Play is not just for kids.

"YOU KNOW YOU'RE IN LOVE WHEN YOU CAN'T FALL ASLEEP BECAUSE REALITY IS FINALLY BETTER THAN YOUR DREAMS."
—DR. SEUSS

One of the biggest struggles in marriage is when two people are trying to communicate, yet they are speaking a different language. A lot is being said, but very little is being understood. The majority of us choose whom we marry, and I'm guessing it's for a good reason, so it's not like we're stuck with someone whom we have nothing in common. We want to be together, or at least at one time we did. Unless we develop good communication now, we may be in a relationship with both parties feeling extremely frustrated and alone.

We're all about making the "journey" a fun ride, so in order to avoid as much communication frustration as possible, I want to share a technique a counselor shared with Mark and me when we were in a rough spot.

It's a communication tool that does take effort and time, and it's not needed for every discussion. But if you ever find yourself in a stalemate, this may help.

BLA BLA B

BLA BLA BLA

BLA BLA BLA

DAY 1:

(I told you it takes effort and time.) Person 1 has 30 minutes to share her side of the story. It's not to be a time of "accusation." *You fat, lazy turd. You spent all the extra money on getting your back waxed!*

Instead, point out facts, and share how it made you feel or affected you. *I understand you wanted to have your back waxed for vacation, but by spending all the money in our savings to do so, the kids and I no longer have any money to buy bathing suits.*

Person 2 doesn't respond; they only listen to Person 1. After Person 1 is finished sharing, Person 2 then repeats what they heard and Person 1 either will affirm or correct it.

DAY 2:

Person 2 now responds: *I'm sorry I spent all the money. I didn't realize you and the kids needed bathing suits. I wanted to look HOT for you on the beach. Ever since cousin Billy Bob called me Hairyback Harold in grade school, I've been insecure of my back hair.*

Person 1 listens and repeats her interpretation.

DAY 3:

Persons 1 and 2 work together on a solution. Person 1: *It was wrong of me to spend $500 to get my back waxed without first talking to you about it. I will cancel my Botox appointment so you and the kids can buy bathing suits.* **Person 2:** *Thank you, my love! You are the best husband in the world!*

I know it's a long process, but the beauty of it is the time. Instead of developing your argument as the other gives his side, you truly listen because you know you will need to repeat it in 30 minutes. Also, I've found as I wait for my moment to shine and give my side of the story, I sometimes wake up that morning realizing my point was kind of frivolous and no longer irked me.

Only things that were important remained.

This may not work for everyone and/or all situations, but it's critical that we continue to work together on our forms of communication. There is nothing more lonely than traveling through life with a partner and feeling like you're not being heard. It will be worth the effort. And remember, it's not just important that *you* are heard. It's equally important that you are hearing what your spouse or significant other is saying as well.

SEASONS CHANGE, ROLES CHANGE.

Each year brings a different set of circumstances. A husband may lose his job, requiring him to be a stay-at-home dad for a season.

The stay-at-home mom may decide to return to the workplace either by choice or for need.

Kids grow up and move out.

One spouse may get the dream job on the other side of the country. You move and you leave your job and friends behind.

Your parent gets sick and needs full-time care.

So many things can throw our perfectly orchestrated life into a mosh pit.

As we age, there's a tendency to get set in our ways, but we need to hold on to these loosely. Remember, life is not about getting everything "we" want done. It's about living and enjoying it together.

"LOVE RECOGNIZES NO BARRIERS. IT JUMPS HURDLES, LEAPS FENCES, PENETRATES WALLS TO ARRIVE AT ITS DESTINATION FULL OF HOPE."

—MAYA ANGELOU

SEE THE POTENTIAL IN YOUR SIGNIFICANT OTHER.

In the early years of our marriage, Mark and I tested the publishing waters. He had two books published and, in the process, began realizing ways publishing could be done better. Not long after this, he began talking about starting our own publishing company.

He could see my uncertainty and would say, "Don't worry, I'm only talking."

But we kept talking about it, a lot.

One day, we were over at the home of some friends, eating dinner. Mark shared his dream, and my dear friend, who was an editor, squealed, "If you do, we'll help you! I'll help edit!" They gave us the support we needed on so many levels to believe it was a possibility.

The dream grew and more friends supported us, and before I knew it, we were a company. It wasn't easy, and there have been a lot of scary lows and even more mind-blowing highs as God blessed and walked us through this journey.

Here's the thing: When Mark began talking about the company, I thought he was just blowing smoke (more likely that he had been smoking something). I didn't think it was anything we could ever do. But, over the years, as he continued to talk, I could see he had really thought this out. It was a passion that was not leaving him. In fact, the passion appeared to grow. He even sacrificed his time, working two part-time jobs, in addition to his full-time job, in order to make sure our family didn't suffer.

The time came when both of us needed to quit our present jobs in order to work on the company full-time.

I had a choice. I had to believe in him and support him, or we could take the easy route and continue living our present life.

The fact that you're able to read this book is because my awesome husband had a dream, and he went after it. We went after it, together.

Fear of failing squashes the dreams inside many of us. If only we had someone to believe in us—whether it be a spouse, a friend, a colleague—to encourage us.

Mark was created to be an entrepreneur. He wasn't truly happy doing anything else. He's happier. I'm happier. The children are happier.

There is a dream with lots of potential within you and your spouse. Look for it, and help them see it. There will be risks, and it will cost you something. But that is a huge part of dreams. Dreams worth pursuing always involve that possibility of failure, but when they come true, it's all the more rich because you took that chance.

Consider This:

- Daily life can wear us down, and if we're not careful, life becomes all work and no play. Pick a day on the calendar and invite your spouse to a day of play. Leave the gadgets behind, and focus solely on one another. Be open-minded and patient. It may take some time to deprogram the mindset of "needing to get stuff done."

- How do you handle conflict with your spouse? Are you *hearing* what he is saying? Communication is vital to keep a relationship healthy. Next time you have a disagreement, make full effort to hear the other side and acknowledge it.

CHAPTER 5
CHILDREN: HOW DID THIS HAPPEN?

> "I DON'T REMEMBER WHO SAID THIS, BUT THERE REALLY
> ARE PLACES IN THE HEART YOU DON'T EVEN KNOW EXIST
> UNTIL YOU LOVE A CHILD."
> —ANNE LAMOTT

There was a time in my life when I wasn't sure I wanted to have kids. That sounds a bit harsh to say, but, growing up, my mom cared for other people's kids during the day. There were always a lot of kids at our house, and I basically grew up in a day care.

But all that changed when Mark and I married. I could think of nothing better than starting a family together. When I was pregnant with Noah, I'd stand in front of a mirror, holding one of his little outfits over my shoulder, my arms aching to hold him in person. When he was born, I felt as if my whole life I had been waiting to meet him.

Mark and I used to argue over who got to hold him.

Close to Noah's first birthday, my heart ached again. This time, I had an uncontrollable urge for a little girl. My sister was pregnant with my niece, and, as I shopped for her baby gift, I bawled in the store, begging God for a girl. I'm sure I made the other customers nervous.

The next week, Mark, Noah, and I went on a beach vacation together. Each day, I'd take a walk down the beach. Once, I saw a little girl playing in the sand with her parents, and my heart cried…literally. Little did I know that I was already pregnant with Anastasia.

She's been my best little girlfriend ever since.

Our kids are my jewels!

I didn't have kids until my mid-30s, so all those years watching my mom run her childcare and my sister and brother-in-law raise their family, I had *plenty* of opinions and saw numerous behaviors I would never let my children do.

Boy, was I WRONG.

All it took was me bringing my children home from the hospital to realize the error in my thinking.

There are a few pieces of advice that I've found in parenting to be forever true, and they are: keep an open mind, pray like crazy, and always give love first.

I want my kids to be a part of my journey—in other words, I want them to be pleasant to be around, AND I want them to enjoy being around me as well. My heart's desire is for Mark and me to be their number one cheerleaders, their number one advisers. I want them to have a great work ethic. I want for them to know and to fulfill their dreams. I want them to know God. I want them to be happy.

You see all those "I wants"?

Even if what *I'm* "wanting" for them is pure, if I'm not careful, I'll turn into a control freak. Half the fun in our personal journey is figuring it out as we go along. I don't want to rob them of that piece. They deserve that freedom, and I feel they will be better for it in the long run (even though it may be painful for me to watch in the process).

So, once again, I must keep an open mind.

"THE TROUBLE WITH BEING A PARENT IS THAT BY THE TIME YOU ARE EXPERIENCED, YOU ARE UNEMPLOYED."

—UNKNOWN

KEEP OUR
EARS OPEN
IN ORDER TO
HEAR WHAT
THEY SAY.

Noah, our oldest child, has a quiet and sweet spirit about him. He's submissive unless it is a strong wrong. If I'm not careful, it's easy for me to overrun him.

When he was younger, in my stress, I'd bark out commands to both kids, trying to get as much done as possible. "I need you guys to clean your rooms and your bathroom before dinner." "Bring down your dirty laundry." "Go get ready for climbing."

Noah is also a lot like me. He gets distracted easily.

One day, after shouting out my demands, I climbed the stairs and saw him playing with a piece of paper on his floor. "Noah! I told you to clean your room!"

"I, uh, I, I was…"

"No you're not. Now clean it!"

Later that night, as we put him to bed, he began crying because he missed his Oma and Opa who lived in Virginia. Turns out, the paper he was playing with was a letter his Oma had written him.

"Why didn't you tell me, honey?"

"I tried, but you wouldn't listen."

He was right. I didn't give him a chance to explain because, in my frustration, I immediately accused him of not doing what I had asked of him. I didn't give him much of a chance to explain. But why did he not try harder and let me know what was going on? My guess…he was scared of me.

Between the two of our kids, one will *flight* and the other will *fight*, so I have to train my ear to hear when they really need to speak. Don't get me wrong, I'm not a fool, and I know kids know how to work the system in their favor, but I want to be wise and aware when there is a deeper issue that needs addressing.

This is hard for us parents. There is so much on our plates (which is why it's good to have a smaller plate!) that we have to rush through our parenting and miss out on teaching moments.

Noah's passive personality causes him to often be overlooked, but there is a lot of wisdom in that kid. It's important for him to learn how to speak up for himself, communicate his thoughts, defend another. But, if I scare that out of him, something that is beautiful about his personality could become a weakness.

He's older now and does a much better job defending himself to me (hello, teenage years). And I've become a better listener over the years (hello, getting too old and tired to fight back). We still have progress to make, but I'm doing my best to keep my ears open.

"YOUR CHILDREN NEED YOUR PRESENCE MORE THAN YOUR PRESENTS."
—JESSE JACKSON

ALWAYS BE PRESENT.

Years ago, I was at a writer's conference. One of the speakers was the author Liz Curtis Higgs. She shared a piece of parenting wisdom that has stayed with me ever since.

When her kids were teenagers, a friend told her, "Now that your kids are older and more independent, you'll have more time to travel and work on developing your speaking career." But she didn't agree. She told her friend that she felt it was more important for her to be home while they were teenagers.

"You never know when a teenager will speak. I want to make sure I'm around when they do."

Liz continued working while they were teens. She just didn't say "yes" to every speaking opportunity. She held that off until they were out of the home.

Many moms work out of the home, whether by choice or need, and there's not much margin to change this. But I think these words carry a lot of value in our world of electronic gadgets.

When we are present, we need to be *fully* present. This is easier said than done. Mark and I work on our computers all hours of the day, but when my kids enter the room to talk to me, I need to make sure I don't roll my eyes or use any other body language that makes them feel they are an interruption.

Children are not interruptions. They are blessings.

Growing up, my family went through a tough time financially. My mom ran her day care out of our home because she wanted to be home with us. My father worked full-time during the day and, at night, he ran a desktop publishing business. Whenever he had a free moment, he'd be at work on the computer.

However, I always knew he was there for me because ANY time I wanted or needed to talk to him, all I had to say was, "Dad?"

He'd immediately turn away from the computer, face me, and have a genuine smile on his face as if he were happy to spend time with me. He welcomed me into his presence.

I never felt I had interrupted him, and I was never hesitant to approach him because I knew I was more important than his work. To this day, I cry thinking about this. He left that big of an impression on me. I knew he loved and treasured me.

We may not be able to cut back our hours. We may not be able to work from home. But, whenever we are in the presence of our children, they need to know they are treasured, and they are loved.

"ALWAYS BE NICE TO YOUR CHILDREN BECAUSE THEY ARE THE ONES WHO CHOOSE YOUR REST HOME."
—PHYLLIS DILLER

HAVE AN OPEN DOOR POLICY.

My daughter, Anastasia, loves hosting people. She loves it when we have guests and especially if these guests are family or her own friends. Even more, she loves throwing a good party.

She's a good decorator as well. When she was three years old, I found a beaded toy necklace around the base of the toilet in the kids' bathroom. I was about to pick it up when she stopped me, "No, Mommy. I put it there to make the toilet look pretty."

It did make it look pretty. I had never thought of an ornate toilet before, but another side of me thought of her brother and his inability to always "hit the mark" when using the bathroom. She was so proud of it that I left it. Luckily, it was only a matter of time before she, too, saw the issue and we tossed the pretty necklace in the trash.

This fall, she asked me if we could host a Halloween party. I love to host, but I'm more of a small group kind of hostess. I don't have much experience throwing large parties, so my mind doesn't naturally think of all the details involved when hosting a large number of people.

I told her I'd think about it, hoping she'd forget. She didn't.

I told her we'd need to check with her friends, they may have other plans for Halloween. They didn't.

So, I finally agreed.

The next month, she and I spent hours researching decoration ideas, drink ideas, food ideas. We decorated the outside of the house. We decorated the inside. We sent out invitations and, bit by bit, it all began to fall into place.

The party was a blast. The kids goofed off. The parents hung out. The girls spent the night.

The next morning, I was a queen in the eyes of my daughter. She thanked me over and over for the next week. This party meant more to her than I had realized.

Growing up, I never liked to throw parties because I didn't like being the center of attention. I was shy. But my parents always had our door open for any of my friends to hang out with us. There were a handful of homes that we'd house hop between during the summer, and this was how I enjoyed my time with my friends. I have very fond memories from this time.

Only difference between Anastasia and me is that she thanked me. I don't think I ever considered the need to thank my parents.

It is a valuable investment to open the doors to your children's friends. It doesn't matter the size and/or niceness of the home. As long as they feel loved and welcomed (and there are good snacks), they will come. Our old house was a ghetto house we bought as a fixer upper. We never got around to fixing it up because we started our business instead, and that took all of our extra cash.

I was always embarrassed when my kids' friends visited—mainly because I was embarrassed for their parents to see it. But one of my son's friends, who has a really nice house, walked in and said, "I love coming here."

I realized then, it's not the house, it's the home (and the snacks) that attracts people. You don't need to have a home off of the pages of HGTV. As long as people feel welcomed and are among friends, they will love being in your home.

Opening your doors to your kids' friends will take work. It will cost you money (snack food and replacing broken dishes). Yes, it's only a matter of time before someone does something stupid there—they are kids. But you're providing another safe place for their friends, which will also provide one for your child. And, unfortunately, there are fewer safe places for kids these days.

I don't need to worry about having a perfect house. My focus should be on making it feel like home to all who enter its door.

"IT IS EASIER TO BUILD STRONG CHILDREN THAN TO REPAIR BROKEN MEN."
—FREDERICK DOUGLASS

LEARN FROM OTHER PARENTS.

Years ago, Noah and his friends were into video games. With his own money, he had bought a particular one that had just come out. However, the reviews were mixed on the age appropriateness of it, so I was on the fence.

I had trouble sleeping that night, worrying over if I was selling out or being overly protective.

"God, what do I do?"

A while back, I had seen an interview with a politician who would have his kids write out their arguments in order to help them process their thoughts. As I fought sleep that night, I remembered this story, and it birthed an idea.

The next day, Mark and I had a meeting with Noah and told him that we weren't sure if he could keep the video game. "What?! But you told me earlier I could, and I spent my own money."

"Noah, your point of view is important, and there are times that Dad and I will be wrong. If your opinion is correct, you should be able to convince us you are right. But, when you whine, my mind shuts off, and it's hard for me to hear what you are saying."

I went on to explain that, if he was willing, he could write a proposal (sometimes it sucks having parents as publishers). If he did a good job convincing us in the proposal, we would reconsider allowing him to play the game.

To earn the right to play the game, his proposal needed to include:

- An opening paragraph stating what he wanted and a brief statement stating why.

- He would orally present his argument to us.

- Three points defending his point of view. A minimum of two had to be from research, but the more points the better.

- A concluding paragraph summarizing his desire and points.

- A code of conduct—what was expected from all parties, and what would happen if these rules were not followed.

- A place for all parties to sign and date.

To be honest, there was a part of me that thought I had an easy win. Noah is a bright kid, but he'll do his best to avoid anything that has the appearance of schoolwork.

I was wrong!

He worked the whole day researching and refining his points. This obviously was important to him. His presentation blew us away. It was organized well, and his points showed he had fully thought through his belief system. His protocol was fair for both sides. Mark and I added a couple amendments, but in the end, we signed the contract, and it worked beautifully. Only one time I had to remind him of the contract, and he immediately responded.

I know this sounds extreme. I felt the same when I heard the idea from the politician. But here is why we did it:

- I realized my overreacting made Noah feel I didn't respect his opinion. The last thing I wanted to do was anything that would hurt his self-esteem and our relationship.

- I hoped it would help him learn how to develop an argument without whining.

- It would be a good writing and research practice. Being in publishing, we see this is a dying art.

- It was a reminder, as I mentioned above, for both sides to develop listening skills.

- It would show him the benefit of taking time to evaluate and develop his own thoughts instead of reacting out of emotion.

Yes, it was a lot of work, especially for Noah, and is not something that will work for all, but it did for Noah in this instance. We've never had to use it again. But, developing certain skill sets and character are worth it. It's easier to put the time in now, helping them to develop into quality men and women, than paying thousands of dollars later in therapy bills.

None of us have all of the answers, but we need to be open to other options.

"YOU CAN LEARN MANY THINGS FROM CHILDREN. HOW MUCH PATIENCE YOU HAVE, FOR INSTANCE."
—FRANKLIN P. ADAMS

BYE-BYE, ENTITLEMENT.

"LOVE IS THAT CONDITION IN WHICH THE HAPPINESS OF ANOTHER PERSON IS ESSENTIAL TO YOUR OWN."
—ROBERT HEINLEIN

Unless you've been living in a cave for the past decade, you're probably aware that our culture is dealing with an attitude of entitlement. I don't want to attach this solely to one generation, for I believe it's something many of us deal with on some level. However, I do feel our younger generations manifest it more, mainly because of the way we've raised them.

Our country has been blessed, and whether our annual salary is $20,000 or $500,000, we are fortunate to have systems, laws, and organizations to take care of us.

Our mantra has now become, "It's *my* right!" We view this through how it affects us individually instead of as a community or a country.

Please don't shut me off. I'm not about to get political. I do agree there are many injustices that need to change. We live in an imperfect society. All societies are imperfect, and we have a lot of work to do.

My issue is with entitlement. How are we going to move forward if we look at everything through the eyes of, "How will this affect me?"

When we lived in Germany, I was in language school. One day, the teacher assigned us an exercise of writing a letter. The scenario: We had just stayed at a hotel and the room was dirty and the staff was rude. We were to write a letter of complaint and then offer a solution.

The other students in the class were mostly from Europe. I was the only American, and another was from Japan.

We read our letters out loud to the class. In mine, I had complained about the health hazards of a dirty room, and for a solution, I asked for a refund and a free night in the hotel to be used in the future. Others in the class asked for similar kinds of reimbursements.

Except for my Japanese friend.

The beginning of her letter was similar to ours, but instead of asking for a refund, she gave the hotel suggestions of changes they could make in order to make it more pleasant for other guests in the future.

Our teacher noticed the difference in her letter right away and said, "Over the years of doing this exercise, I've seen this common thread. In the Japanese culture, they don't seek reward for themselves, they seek better for the common good of their society."

It was a slap in the face, for I had asked for more than anyone else in the room. It revealed to me that I, too, carry the attitude, *It's my right.* "I paid for this room and you gave me crappy service, so you need to give me a new car!"

Okay, I'm not that bad, but it is an attitude that I carry, and I'm passing it down to my kids.

Being business owners, we've had to deal head on with the issue of entitlement, and it's been painful at times. The knee jerk reaction is to only hire old people, but I don't think we'd stay in business too long. Have you seen a group of 50 plus year olds try to figure out social media?!

We don't want to live like that, nor run our business like that. The younger generation is filled with incredibly talented people. We need all generations, and I believe they need us as well.

Entitlement is in all of us, and it's my job to not pass it down to my children.

How do I do this? I'm not exactly sure. Like everything new in life, I guess we need to start with baby steps.

Teach them to respect the older generations. The mature crowd may not know how to use certain gadgets or know certain apps, but there is a lot of life-earned wisdom in them. If they listen, they can avoid a lot of pain.

Teach them to respect everyone, regardless of their skin color, nationality, religion, education, or socio-economic class. We are all God's children. We all have a purpose. We all deserve respect. We all need to be loved.

Teach them to look beyond their own bubble. There is a suffering world out there. They are a part of the human race, and therefore need to live and respond to the needs of others—not just their own.

Teach them the value of hard work, even though sometimes work is not fun (e.g., cleaning their nasty bathroom), but it needs to be done. So put down the phone that *we* paid for (man, I really need to stop barking), and clean up your mess.

Help them find their passions and discover what they are good at and move in that direction. Just because their friends are good at something doesn't mean they need to put their energies there as well. They need to find *their* area(s) of gifting.

Teach them to move. Staring at a screen all day is good for no one. (Believe me, I know. I've been doing it for 11 hours a day as I write this book, and I ain't purdy right now!) Endorphins from moving will fuel their hearts and minds toward good. Our bodies were created to move.

Teach them to volunteer. Help them find that soft spot in their hearts (it's there in all of them, although it may be hard to believe sometimes). It may be children, or animals, or refugees, or elderly, or homeless. Once they know what melts their heart, find a way for them to volunteer in this area. It's more likely to stick if it fuels a passion innately in them.

Teach them by modeling. I'm guilty of having the bug of entitlement in me. We all probably have some due to living in our culture. Be honest with them, and let them see that you're aware of your mistakes and model your attempts of making a change. Vulnerability travels deep and fast.

Okay, my friends, in the words of the late, great Michael Jackson, let's "start with the man (hot woman) in the mirror," and the ~~stubborn~~ beautiful children in our homes.

"LOVE ME WHEN I LEAST DESERVE IT, BECAUSE THAT'S WHEN I REALLY NEED IT."
—SWEDISH PROVERB

Consider This:

- We talked earlier about *important* versus *urgent*. Our children should always feel they are more important than the urgent distractions in our life. Our time each day may be limited, but we need to proactively be present, especially with our teenagers.

We never know when they will talk. Personalize this. What ways can you be more present for your children?

- Entitlement is a curse in our culture. We can't just blame it on one generation. It's in all of us. Are you modeling it to your children? If so, begin with small changes in the words you use when frustrated. Take action to make changes that will benefit others, not just yourself. Plant flowers in a common space in your neighborhood. Pick up trash around the playground. Small steps like these will help train their brains to think of others.

CHAPTER 6

PARENTS: I'M SANDWICHED, AND WE ARE OUT OF PEANUT BUTTER

> ## "IT IS NOT HOW MUCH YOU DO, BUT HOW MUCH LOVE YOU PUT INTO THE DOING."
> ### —MOTHER TERESA

What is the "sandwiched generation"?

What is the sandwiched generation? It has nothing to do with a turkey and brie panini, although that sounds incredible right now!

Many of us are part of the pulled in every-which-way sort—a generation of people who are raising our own children, but who are also caring for our aging parents. Generally, we're in our 40s to 60s but can also include younger or older. You may be caring for your parents full-time or part-time. They may be living in your home or across the country and may or may not be living independently.

You are in the middle, caring for both, at times feeling as if you're oozing out of the sides like a squished peanut butter and jelly sandwich.

There have always been generations of people who have cared for multiple generations—the issue now is the size of it. We are having children later and our parents are living longer, so it will only continue to grow, and, before we know it, our children will be "sandwiched." (All the more motivation for me to quit barking at them. I need to make it so they'll put me up in a nice place.)

We're facing new dilemmas. Do we bring our parents into *our* homes? Do we hire others to care for them in *their* homes? Do we place them in a care facility? What if our parents are not very nice people? (I'm not talking about you, Mom and Dad!) But it's true, I'm blessed to have awesome parents, but some parents out there are just plain mean and did bad things to you. How do you deal with that? Do you overlook that to care for them, or is it too much to let go?

There's a lot to think about.

It affects decisions about the future. Do you move to be closer to your parents? Do you buy a house with a ground floor bedroom?

Both sets of our parents are independent and healthy, but when buying our current home, we took them into consideration. We moved four blocks away from Mark's parents, and we bought a home that had a ground floor bedroom next to a full bath with a walk-in shower for my parents to use when they visit or if they ever move in with us. Mark may accuse me of using this tactic to buy a bigger house, but I know better.

Elder care is not cheap either. The costs can go from $20,000 to over $100,000 a year, depending on whether it's part-time, in-home health care, or a full-time nursing home. My guess is it will only increase.

The details alone are overwhelming, not accounting for the emotional and financial stress. If we're not careful, we only see the costs and forget that we're talking about Mom and Dad, our stepmother, our stepfather, our grandmother, our grandfather, aunts and uncles. People who poured love into us, who provided for us. People who deserve love.

But we also have children, spouses, significant others who need our love and attention as well. We don't want to neglect them.

Who takes first priority?

It's a balancing act. The problem is we are the first generation to be faced with being sandwiched at this magnitude for this long. There's not an older generation who modeled it to us. Years ago, fewer women worked out of the home, having more time to care for aging parents. Not meaning to sound morbid, but parents didn't live as long, many dying in their 60s or 70s.

"FAMILY IS NOT AN IMPORTANT THING. IT'S EVERYTHING."
—MICHAEL J. FOX

WHAT DO
WE DO?

As I mentioned before, my parents are still married and going strong. However, my mother had a mild heart attack and stroke this past year. She and my dad live in Virginia, and I live in Idaho (not to be confused with Iowa or Ohio... don't you love my Idahoan humor?). She had a triple by-pass surgery, and I'm happy to say she did great and is on her road to recovery. But her situation did give me a glimpse into what it feels like to be "sandwiched."

Once we learned she needed surgery, my sister, broth-er, and I congregated around her. The first surgery was a heart catheterization that revealed she needed the triple bypass. I flew out to be with her on two separate occa-sions, each trip being seven to nine days. The first was mostly for moral support as we all absorbed the blow of her heart attack and stroke. My second trip was to help prepare her and get their house ready for her to recover from her surgery.

There is no doubt I was supposed to be there on both occasions. They needed me, and I needed to be with them. It was the right thing to do—what I wanted to do— no question. However, when I returned home, I saw that Mark and the kids needed me as well. Mark missed a lot of work due to covering the kids and their activities, homework, etc. He did a wonderful job, but his work and the company suffered because of it, adding a lot of stress to him and others.

So, what do you do? I felt guilty if I stayed home. I felt guilty if I left home. Now I feel guilty that my siblings, who live closer, are doing most of the work. No matter what, someone feels neglected. But all are equally important.

I'm just now entering this phase of life, but I see this is an area of growing concern for many of us in the future.

Many of you are dealing with the same emotions. Some have it worse. Your parents are overseas, and there's a visa issue. For others, your parents are taking advantage of your help and being extra needy. Or you try to help, but they reject it due to dementia, or just being plain hard-headed. They make bad choices, causing your head to spin and leaving you to clean up their messes.

Your own home could be unstable with a broken marriage, a special needs child, a sick spouse. The lists are endless.

There's no easy one-answer fix-all. Most of this generation is just in survival mode, trying to figure it out as they go.

I went to Facebook, and I asked my friends and followers for advice. So many of you had beautiful advice to share, and I send many thanks to all of you who took the time to reply to share your wisdom with me.

Most of you sent me personal messages with details of your story. Small details were different, but they amazingly overlapped.

These words and advice informed and encouraged me, and I hope they will do the same for you:

Take care of yourself. Time is limited when you're sandwiched in-between caring for your children and your parents. You're already working on a deficit. But this is a must. If you're not healthy, you won't be a healthy caregiver.

Eat right. Exercise, or at the least, move regularly. Take naps when your children or parents nap. Forget about the laundry, instead, sleep! Monitor your own health and keep up on your doctor appointments. I know the last thing you want to do is visit another doctor, but this, too, is a must.

Take shifts with other family members or health care workers. Yes, this is your mother or your father, and you may feel no one can care for them as well as you, but for your own sanity, share the load. Your brother, Bubba, may not know how to boil water and leaves the toilet seat up or your sister, Bertha, curses like a sailor (and dates a lot of them, too), and you fear they'll forget to give your mom her meds. Give them a chance to step up to the plate. If you fear for your mom's safety, hire out some help. Talk to churches or neighbors to find volunteers to sit with her while you take a break.

Whatever you do, do not feel guilty that someone else is helping. You cannot do it 24/7. It's not healthy for you, your children, your spouse, or your parents.

When my mom left the hospital after her heart attack, I went home with her while my sister drove back to Atlanta to tend to her family. This gave her a five-day break while I helped Dad care for Mom. When it was time for me to return to Idaho, she drove up to cover me. She was refreshed, a new person. She needed that break. I experienced the same when I returned a few weeks later. Having time off rejuvenates you, and you're able to give 100 percent.

Have your kids help out with the caregiving. If your kids are in grade school, there are things they can do to help out. They can sit and read to their grandparent. They can help feed them (if stroke and swallowing are not an issue). They can talk with them, watch TV with them while you clean, do laundry (or take a nap…maybe). Don't leave them alone with them, but a younger child can alert you if there is an issue. "Mom! Grandpa is trying to pee in the plant again!"

Remember what we just talked about…entitlement! We don't want to raise kids who feel it's beneath them to care for their own (especially when they will be caring for us one day)! We need to model this love and caregiving to them. A great way to do this is to have them be part of it.

My sister and brother brought their young children with them to visit my mom. It was *pure* medicine for her soul! Nothing got her up moving and talking faster than having my niece and nephew in her presence. Not all elderly care for children, but if they do, it will revive them.

Process it with others. Talk to family or friends. Vent. Share your struggles and emotions and don't feel guilty about them. They are normal, and you are human. Find a support group. They are popping up everywhere as more and more experience this struggle. One of my friends who messaged her story to me told me afterwards that the small act of typing it out helped her process her emotions. Sharing is good therapy.

Talk in advance to your parents. What are their expectations? Are their wills up to date? What is their insurance? Do they want to remain at home? Are they willing to have aid workers help them at home? Would they want to live with you (some may prefer your sibling—gasp!), or would they prefer a nursing home? You may be surprised what they say. "No way in Hades can I live with you as long as you're married to that scumbag." (I'm not speaking from experience, of course!)

Look into senior care insurance. It's recommended to do so when you enter your 50s (which means for a lot of us, it's time!). See if your parent is eligible. A friend, who is a past insurance agent, shares this: "In regards to yourself, get Disability Insurance if you are working. Get Long-Term Care Insurance around the age of 60. Get a Power of Attorney, Will, Trust, and a Health Directive with your parents, and do it right away."

Get their banking, investments, and any other financial records now before a tragedy strikes. Get organized.

Bring in outside help. Hire a housekeeper to help clean their house. Hire a college student to sleep overnight. As I mentioned before, seek out churches and other non-profits who may provide volunteers who will come sit with your dad while you run to the grocery store, or get your nails done, or go to your child's soccer game, or just plain relax at the pool with your kids.

Send group updates. Friends and family are wonderful, and they want to check in, ask how to help and how to pray. My suggestion is to send out group updates on Facebook, or a blog, or a site like CaringBridge.org. It takes a lot of time to send out individual messages, so it helps to cover all the bases at one time. Leave regular updates about your loved one and even suggestions of how others can help. Be bold. You *have* not because you *ask* not. Ask for meals, volunteers to sit with your loved one. Ask for yard help, house cleaning, grocery shopping. You may get a great response.

Talk with your employer. Ask if flexible hours or working from home are a possibility. Some may even offer benefits. If necessary, and you qualify, you may be able to take unpaid leave for a short period and have your job secured under the Family Medical Leave Act (FMLA). Not all private sector employees are covered under the FMLA, so another reason to talk with your employer.

Don't question yourself. Don't plague your mind with I should have done this, or I could have done that, or I wish I would have been there. Do the best you can, and leave it at that. You have two families you are caring for, and you can't do everything. Remind yourself you are doing a wonderful job. It's hard, and it's impossible to do everything. Be open and honest with your children, your parents, your spouse…and yourself.

Work together as a family. You'll be stronger in the end, and your heart will increase as you are filled with more love.

"CAREGIVING OFTEN CALLS US TO LEAN INTO LOVE WE DIDN'T KNOW POSSIBLE."
—TIA WALKER

HELPFUL
SOURCES.

Here is a list of a few agencies that I found during my research that either provide or will help you locate services in your area.

Eldercare.gov—a public service of the U.S. Administration on Aging that will help you locate elder care in your local area.

N4a.org—their mission is to assist the elderly in living with dignity. There is a link on this site that gives information on caregiving, insurance, transitions (movement between health care practitioners and their settings or the care needs of the patient change), etc.

Caring.com—this site primarily assists in finding proper living for the elderly from assisted living to memory care to nursing home to in-home care.

Visitingangels.com—is an elder care franchised agency that assists you with finding in-home care in your area.

Parentgiving.com—a site where you can shop for products needed for the elderly—showers, walkers, commodes, bedrails, etc.

I wish I could give you more, but hopefully this is a start.

"WE CAN DO NO GREAT THINGS; ONLY SMALL THINGS WITH GREAT LOVE."
—MOTHER TERESA

Consider This:

- If your parents are still living, begin talking with them about future care. This may be an uncomfortable conversation, but taking care of small details now will help you to make other decisions in the future.

- If you are a parent, begin taking steps to make this easier for your children. Look into elder care insurance. Make sure you have one location where you keep important documents, such as wills, bank information, etc.

- If you are a friend or family member, reach out to one another. Offer to parent-sit or babysit or carpool one day a month or one day a week. Being "sandwiched" is a new norm for our society, but it doesn't have to be a horrible thing. It can be a beautiful way of bringing *community* back into our independent-living culture.

SECTION

3

OPTIMAL HEALTH

> ## "EVERYTHING SLOWS DOWN WITH AGE, EXCEPT THE TIME IT TAKES CAKE AND ICE CREAM TO REACH YOUR HIPS."
> ### —JOHN WAGNER

We're going to have more fun in this section. It's not quite so heavy, but I use that term loosely.

It's amazing the effect that aging has on our body and mind. Anything that is good slows down, and anything bad speeds up. The beautiful thick eyebrows I plucked to death in the 80s have migrated down my face and magically appear overnight on my chin.

Only problem is that my failing eyes aren't able to see them in my bathroom mirror. I only notice them in my car, when I look in my rearview, on my way to an appointment! I really should keep a pair of tweezers in my car, but I keep forgetting.

Oh yeah, the mind. I almost forgot to mention how my memory and focus are, uh, something. I can't think of the word. All I know is my mind doesn't always work right!

I used to remember names and faces in my 30s. Then, in my 40s, I recognized faces, but I would struggle recalling the names. I was grateful because eventually the names would surface. Now I can meet someone and they tell me they met me at Bobby Sue's birthday party. At first I think they are messing with me until Mark comes up and picks up the conversation where we left off, supposedly from the party.

Am I going crazy?

My family assures me I'm not...well, to my face. Who knows what they are saying behind my back. After I went postal on them a month back, I notice now that whenever I walk in the room, they part, like the Red Sea, and offer me their seat. "Just smile and nod. Smile and nod. If you counter her, it will only get worse."

Maybe it's from lack of sleep. Or maybe it's my aching back. When you're tired and in pain, you don't feel like going for a run. If you feel that bad *before* the run, imagine what you'll feel like *after?!*

It's amazing what a hairy chin, foggy brain, sleep deprivation, and an aching body can do to your emotional state! Oh, the flabby thighs. Almost forgot those. All I want to do is stay indoors in my sweats and watch old *Friends* reruns. Then I see how cute and perky Rachel is, and I'm more depressed.

This may be a slightly dramatized version of my past year (emphasis on slightly), but I have experienced all of this. I've been proactive in visiting health care professionals, talking with friends, working with trainers, and spending a lot of time reading and praying.

I'm happy to say I'm doing much better. I still have a ways to go, but I'm moving forward, and baby steps are easier to handle when your hips hurt. What I'm about to share is NOT a prescription for the masses (not that I think masses are reading this book). It is purely my own personal story and what has worked for me. I'm sharing this solely to pass on encouragement, in case you struggle with similar issues, in hopes that it might help you figure out your next right step.

Taking care of our bodies and minds is not only important but essential because the two are interconnected in so many ways. If your mind is strong, then you move more. If your body feels good, then your mind is free to create. If your body hurts, then your mind will tense up.

Don't neglect your health. You may be able to live long with bad health, but that is not truly living.

"FIRST YOU FORGET NAMES, THEN YOU FORGET FACES, THEN YOU FORGET TO PULL YOUR ZIPPER UP, THEN YOU FORGET TO PULL YOUR ZIPPER DOWN."
—LEO ROSENBERG

CHAPTER 7

INTERNAL HEALTH: HORMONES, SCHMOREMONES

"NOT SLEEPING, MEMORY LOSS, ANGRINESS AND FRUS-TRATION, PAINS ALL OVER MY BODY AND HOT FLASHES AT LEAST 15 TIMES A DAY. IF I WAS A DOG, I'M SURE I WOULD BE PUT DOWN."

—UNKNOWN

I knew I needed to get back into shape. I had gained 10 pounds in the past year alone, something all my doctors were quick to point out. Once they determined it was not due my thyroid, they gave me the lecture, "You're getting older, and your hormones are changing, so you need to change your lifestyle habits. Maybe cut out the sugar, and limit your alcohol."

It's easy to cut out sugar when you're feeling good (well, not *easy*, but easier). I was tempted to give him a hand gesture and tell him to, "Suck it." However, Boise is a small town, and I knew it would come back to haunt either me or a family member. So, I took the higher road and just smiled and nodded.

I shared with him my struggles with energy and sleep. "I haven't slept well in years." A normal night for me was waking up every two hours. A good night was being able to go back to sleep each time. There were many nights I'd get up and read or work on my computer, getting only a total of three to four hours of sleep.

"Try meditating. Cut out caffeine. Move. You need to move and work out regularly. That will do wonders for you."

I longed to be back in the same shape I was two years prior. I had competed in triathlons and road races. I had infinite energy. Now, each time I went out on a run, my heart would have palpitations, continuously. I would get lightheaded if I didn't stop, and at times came close to passing out.

I wanted to be healthy and have my pre-40s body back, but not if it would cause me to die prematurely and leave my kids without a mom and Mark without his *hot* wife. (If I say, "I'm hot" enough, it may one day come true!)

Don't get me wrong. Mark is an incredible father, but he *really* needs me around as his helpmate. There aren't many women out there willing to silently remove a dirty dust mop pad from the drawer of their clean dish towels because their husband didn't know the difference. I had to think about my kids—and yes, this really did happen!

I went back to the doctor and pushed a little harder. I told him about the heart palpitations and how I was having problems with pain in the largest joints in my thumbs, making it impossible for me to hold a glass. He seemed concerned and immediately ordered tests on my heart and blood work to check for autoimmune diseases.

The blood work and heart tests came back clean, but the x-rays revealed the beginning of osteoarthritis in my hands and some deterioration in my back.

He basically told me the same story, "You're getting older, so diet and strength exercises are important."

For someone already dealing with depression (even though I was still unaware of it at the time), I felt hopeless and fell into a deeper pit—and pits stink in so many ways.

I became more disciplined with my strength workouts, mainly using my body weight, and felt some improvement. I tried to cut out certain inflammatory foods (gluten and dairy) in my diet, even though my doctor told me this wouldn't help with osteoarthritis.

My hands felt better, but the heart issues remained.

Finally, one day I heard a voice in my head telling me to go make an appointment with a holistic physician assistant (PA) I had visited years ago and for me to "do it now." I know this may sound a little freaky to some, but I know it was God directing me.

My health insurance wouldn't cover the visit, but I was desperate. When your heart flutters and beats out of control randomly, it's an uneasy feeling. Last thing I want to do is collapse in public while wearing a dress. I'm sure it would happen on a day I was wearing granny underwear, and some kid would record it on his phone, and it'd end up going viral. My kids would be so proud.

I was so desperate, I was willing to pay out of pocket.

Goodbye fancy overpriced coffee.

The PA was excellent. He spent a lot of time with me talking about my symptoms, lifestyle, diet, exercise, etc. He informed me that not only had I gained weight, but my muscle mass and fat ratio were also bordering an unhealthy state.

Not exactly what I was hoping to hear.

He ordered close to a gallon of blood work, or so it felt, and I miraculously didn't pass out in the process.

A week later, I went back to his office for the results. Here is the gist of what he told me:

- My estrogen was extremely low, "Most men have more estrogen in their bodies than you," he exclaimed. (Hello, chin hair.)

- My progesterone was low.

- My vitamin B12, D, and magnesium were all low.

- My cholesterol was good, but my HDL (good cholesterol) could be a little higher.

- I also showed deficiencies in other areas, which could mean that my body wasn't absorbing the needed vitamins and minerals from my food.

Earlier in his career he had worked in the ER. He told me, "Many women in their 40s would come in thinking they were having a heart attack. We did tests, found nothing wrong, and would send them home telling them it was either stress or in their head. I wish I knew then what I now know."

He went on to explain to me that healthy blood vessels are naturally pliable, but when your hormones are off balance, they lose this pliability and are more hardened. This can raise blood pressure in an otherwise healthy individual and exaggerate other conditions.

I have a mild case of mitral valve prolapse (MVP—not to be confused with Most Valuable Player—a slightly deformed heart valve), so my guess is there is a good chance when I was active or my blood pressure was high due to wacko hormones, it aggravated my MVP.

He prescribed a bio-identical crème-form of estrogen I rub on my abdomen in the morning as well as a higher dose of progesterone I take in pill form at night. He also recommended that I take magnesium at night as it could help with sleep and with my heart palpitations.

"IF YOU'RE LOOKING FOR STABILITY IN YOUR LIFE, BEFRIEND A WOMAN IN MENOPAUSE. SUDDENLY EVERYTHING ELSE IN YOUR LIFE WILL SEEM ROCK-SOLID STABLE."
—UNKNOWN

CHANGE
TAKES TIME.

It's been months since I've been on this new hormone therapy and it's amazing. I actually have been able to work out with my heart feeling few ill effects. This was not an overnight change, but within a week or so, I went from not being able to do any aerobic exercise to being able to walk/jog and ride my bike again.

I'm beginning to feel like my old self. I'm still nowhere near my previous level of fitness, but this is huge progress.

It wasn't just my energy, but some of the fogginess in my mind improved as well. When my mom had her stroke, the doctor told her to take vitamin B12, it helps with memory and brain function. Since my blood work showed I was low on B12 as well, I've been proactive in taking this daily, and it has helped.

In the past when I read workout programs, I always ignored the warning, "Please check with a physician before beginning a workout regimen." But now I get it. As we age, there are minor "tweaks" that are needed in our body's chemistry that are unique to us.

We are blessed to have modern medicine to help and also the knowledge of men and women who have studied how food can also help our bodies perform.

Our bodies are holistic. If one part is out of sync, it can have a huge impact on our cardiovascular system, our mental focus, our moods, our energy, etc.

There was a time I would have laughed at the thought of visiting a homeopathic/holistic PA. But now I'm thanking God that there was one nearby who had the insight to help me.

This was the first step I needed to take in order to be able to do any form of aerobic activity. If my mind was not focused and my energy was lacking, I know from personal experience that I will sit on the couch, eat chips, and watch others from the sideline. And, while this is okay sometimes, WE WERE NOT CREATED TO SIT THERE OUR WHOLE LIVES! We were created to move, create, love, be, experience, enjoy, laugh, challenge ourselves, and move forward, all the while making the world a better place.

This is harder to do if we are not healthy.

This was the beginning of my quest to regain my physical fitness and health. What worked for me may not work for you, but start. Take that first step. What are your symptoms? Is it pain? Is it energy? Are you up to date on your well checkups? Talk to friends, ask questions, seek to find that medical professional or dietician who may be able to help you.

Whatever you do, don't delay. Your health is worth it. You are worth it.

"IF PRISON GUARDS WERE MENOPAUSAL WOMEN, THEN WE'D HAVE NO PROBLEM WITH CRIME."
—UNKNOWN

KEEP
SEARCHING
FOR THE RIGHT
DOCTOR.

I first went to my gynecologist with my perimenopause symptoms and then to my primary health care provider with my heart and joint pain. This worked for years until I was full blown into menopause. I needed an expert on hormones as I entered menopause at a younger age than normal. The one-size-fits-all hormone therapy didn't work for me. I needed someone who would help me figure out the correct hormone cocktail. (It sounds lovely when put that way, doesn't it?)

It took years for me to find him. Insurance made it harder as well since some years I had already had my well check up for that year. They wouldn't cover my doctor search. Living in a midsize city, my options were limited, and that can be another hurdle for many.

Talk to friends in your area and find out what has been working for them. Don't be embarrassed. It's something we all will go through, and there's no bravery in doing this alone. It's hard to do, but that doesn't mean you are weak.

I am a believer in exercise, but my experience showed me it's not the "cure all" all the time. If your body chemistry needs help, you need to start first with a health care professional. Exercise and diet were not helping my elevated blood pressure, which didn't drop until I got my hormone levels balanced. Then I was able to begin exercise again and strengthen my heart.

I have dear friends who are against hormone replacement. They have entered and gone through menopause without and had no issues. I applaud them (and secretly wish I were them), but as I mentioned before, our bodies are all different. So just because this worked for me doesn't make it a prescription for all. You may fare better skipping hormone replacement altogether. That is for you and your doctor to decide.

My point, let's not judge others who use hormone replacement, nor judge those who go without it. We all know our bodies better than anyone else. We need to support each other on this part of the journey, no matter which route our body takes us.

What is the next step you need to take?

Don't stall, maybe it's time to step away from the sideline and begin your own journey!

Consider This:

- How is your health? Are you up-to-date on your doctor visits? Don't be like me and let insurance issues cause you to delay. You are worth it. If you are feeling well, it's easier to be a better spouse, parent, worker. Pick up the phone and make that appointment.

- If you're not happy with your doctor, ask around. Talk to friends and co-workers and find recommendations for other doctors.

CHAPTER 8

EMOTIONAL HEALTH: DON'T LOOK AT ME LIKE I'M CRAZY!

> "NOT UNTIL WE ARE LOST DO WE BEGIN
> TO UNDERSTAND OURSELVES."
> —HENRY DAVID THOREAU

Mental and emotional health are topics that have been in the headlines a great deal lately. I'm not talking in regards to the presidential race. (Bad joke?! Just waiting to see if my editor will delete this!)

In the past, if one suffered from mental and emotional health, it was taboo to discuss. It was kept behind closed doors. It was a label, a scarlet letter, something that made you unable or unworthy to work and associate in *normal* society.

What is normal, anyway?

In the past years, many brave souls have opened up about their struggles with depression and anxiety. Thankfully, they have made it easier for those of us who also suffer from bouts of depression.

A little over a year ago, I knew something wasn't right. Was it full-blown depression? Was it just a crisis? Was it a disease?

I don't know. I do know that I woke up each morning dreading the day. Nothing excited me. Nothing motivated me. I only worked out of obligation, not out of passion. I never truly laughed. I only saw my failures. I saw no strengths. I had been hurt that year by a family friend, and my mind obsessed over the negative words he said of me, destroying my self-worth.

At my weakest point, I even wondered if Mark and the kids would be better off without me. My erratic emotions caused outbursts and words that I knew hurt them. Was I doing more damage than good? Would they fare better with someone more stable in their life?

The scary part, no one knew I was dealing with these thoughts. In public, I was always happy and goofing off with people.

But, at night, my mind would wreak havoc in the cave of my skull. "You screwed up again today...You didn't get any chapters written...You call yourself a creative, you can't even focus long enough to write one sentence...What kind of mother snaps at her children like that...You're not smart enough to help Mark run the business..."

The ironic thing is I was clueless to the fact that it could be depression. I felt down, and I knew I was dealing with insecurities. I tried to fight them off, but every success was met with a huge blow. It wasn't until I was "attempting" a run with Mark one day that the reality of my situation came to life.

It was before I had begun my hormone therapy, and I was dealing with the heart palpitations I mentioned above.

I've always dealt with them, due to my MVP, but they had never been on this level before. I had told Mark of my dizzy spells, but I had not communicated the severity of it.

On our run, a dizzy spell hit, and it was so bad I grabbed hold of a fence to keep from falling over. It was the first time Mark had seen me experience one. "Are you all right? Let's sit down."

"No. I'm fine. If I keep walking, it will eventually go away."

Mark was dumbfounded and kept asking me what was going on. Finally, I answered, "This is what my heart does to me every time I run. I'm so tired of it. I can't do anything. I feel as if I'm just 'getting by' with my life until the 'big one' hits and permanently stops my heart. I wish it would hurry up and happen. I'm tired of living like this. I just want to be done with it."

These words articulated everything I had been feeling, but wasn't brave enough to admit.

They silenced both of us as we absorbed their meaning. Mark immediately began encouraging, asking me not to give up. We'd get some help and figure out what was going on with my heart.

We did, and I'm blessed it was something as simple as getting my hormones and certain vitamin and mineral levels balanced (which aided my sleep) for me to feel better. I know there are others who have it deeper and darker and need the aid of medicines and help of other professionals in the medical field. Having a glimpse of that from the inside, I now know it is true, and it is real.

The goal is to find out what you and your body need to make you feel whole again.

I'm sharing my story not to tell you what to do. I have no medical background. I'm telling it to let you know, I get it. It's real, and it's scary. People tell you to snap out of it. Think happy thoughts. Go for a run. But it's not always that easy. We need to get help, and it's okay to reach out.

"THERE IS ONE CONSOLATION IN BEING SICK; AND THAT IS THE POSSIBILITY THAT YOU MAY RECOVER TO A BETTER STATE THAN YOU WERE EVER IN BEFORE."
—HENRY DAVID THOREAU

ARE YOU DEPRESSED, OR ARE YOU JUST DOWN IN THE DUMPS?

As we transition into the next phase of our life, we can get stuck in a rut. It may be depression. It may not be depression, but all we know is that we're not 100 percent ourselves. It could be caused by family dynamics—the kids are getting older and don't need us as much. We may be struggling in our marriage. We may no longer enjoy our careers that fueled us in our youth. They don't give us purpose and make us feel as if we're spinning in circles.

Birthdays can plague us with anxiety as we look back over our life and realize all we have yet to accomplish. We compare our "successes" to others and feel as if we've contributed little to the world.

These and more can leave us feeling down. If we aren't careful, these thoughts can ooze their tentacles into our mind and heart and suffocate any truth and reason out of it. Before we know it, our "down in the dumps" is moving into full-blown depression.

"YOUR PRESENT CIRCUMSTANCES DON'T DETERMINE WHERE YOU CAN GO; THEY MERELY DETERMINE WHERE YOU CAN START."

—NIDO QUBEIN

THE BODY FOLLOWS WHAT THE MIND THINKS.

I don't want to go back to that dark period in my life ever again. So, I've been proactive in keeping my mind in a healthy spot. But it can be a struggle.

Growing up, I had a great aunt who told me I would be pretty IF I got a nose job. Oh, yeah, I was 13 years old at the time. It didn't help that the boys in my class began making nose jokes about me around the same time, "Don't question her, the *nose* knows!" At age 12, my grandmother told me I had fat thighs (hmm...I wonder if that's why I always make jokes about my thighs?)! Luckily, my uncle was in the room and emphatically defended me, "Her legs aren't fat. That's muscle. She's a soccer player. Her strong legs are why she's so good!"

It still makes me cry remembering his words defending me.

We have all been scarred by the spoken words of others or by physical or emotional abuse from others. Just as we're making progress, they never fail to pop up in our mind, haunting us with their lies.

Below are tactics I use to help me when I'm struggling with negative thoughts or am down because of my circumstances or the craziness of life.

Go outside. When we lived in Germany, a friend told me Germans believe you should spend a minimum of one hour a day outside, regardless of the weather. Which would explain why I saw mothers pushing infants in strollers in the snow. Grandmas riding bikes in the rain. Families taking long leisurely walks in the evening.

While writing this book, I've taken five-minute breaks, every hour, to go outside and just sit in the sun. Okay, it would have been healthier if I wasn't sitting, but being in fresh air, absorbing the rays, lifted my spirits and enabled me to focus and continue writing.

Probiotics. The gut is known as the second brain, mainly because the gut lining is made up of hundreds of millions of neurons called the enteric nervous system, which plays a role in producing 30 different neurotransmitters, such as serotonin—chemicals that regulate mood.

Probiotics are the healthy bacteria in our guts. If our healthy bacteria are low, research has shown there is a higher risk of anxiety, depression, and inflammation. Eating fermented (sorry, not talking about beer or wine here) foods, such as yogurt, kefir, sauerkraut, or kimchi, is a natural way to put good bacteria in your gut. Or you could supplement with a nice pricey pill.

Sleep more. Sleep is a key player in mental and emotional health. Arianna Huffington in her book *The Sleep Revolution* says, "Sleep deprivation has been found to have a strong connection with practically every mental health disorder we know of, especially depression and anxiety." It has even been associated with Alzheimer's disease and other forms of dementia.

We need sleep. It affects our productivity, our emotions, our energy, our stress level, and more.

I know it's aggravating to family and friends trying to reach me at night, but I turn off my phone one to two hours before sleep. I either talk with my family or read during this time, but nothing too thought provoking, otherwise my mind won't calm down.

Television is the only problem with this plan, if we don't turn it off early enough at night, I'm reading later, which cuts into my sleep time. I'm working now to cut television out. It's not perfect yet, but it's a work in progress.

I'm still not a great sleeper, but I'm much better than I was in the past.

Limit social media. I love social media. It's a fun way to keep up with friends and share what's going on in your life. But let's be honest, we only post the fun times and the best photos of us. To test this theory, a few years ago, I had my kids take a photo of me at the dinner table, drinking water. The caption was, "Loving life."

It threw everyone into a loop. "What?!...I'm confused...What are you drinking?!" There was a bottle of olive oil on the table near me. One friend even looked up the name on the bottle, trying to figure out if I was drinking something "special." It was hilarious.

My point, the majority of my life is normal, everyday stuff, nothing exciting. Many a time I've looked at other people's posts and thought, "Wow, I want to go on their vacation." "Their kids are going to that school?! I'm falling behind in my parenting." "I want a house like theirs."

It's been shown, unless you're interacting, leaving comments, and "liking" someone's posts, you will leave social media feeling worse than before.

To the contrary, if you like the posts and give people words of encouragement, it will lift your mood.

Move. Take a walk. Ride the bike. Go for a swim. Do some squats. Limit your time sitting, which is the new smoking, so I've been told. It's only a matter of time before they put warnings on chairs, "Prolonged use of this chair will shorten your life."

Get the feel good endorphins moving. Some days it helps me more than taking a nap.

Get together with a friend. It's hard for some to believe this, but I'm a shy person, and it's hard for me to reach out to people. I'm always glad when I do.

There's a reason isolation is a form of torture. We were created to be a community. Spending time with friends, talking, sharing, laughing, praying for one another does wonders for your soul.

Combine this with the previous one (move) and sign up and train for a race with friends. It will make exercise all the more fun and you'll have un-interrupted time to chat.

Start a gratitude journal. Oprah made this popular years ago, and I think it's golden. When I look at and focus on all that I have to be thankful for, I can't help but feel better.

Prayer and meditation. When times are hard, prayer and meditation are usually the last things I want to do—when they are actually what I need the most. It may feel awkward and fake because of my attitude. But when I put the time into praying, reading the Bible, and being still before God, his Spirit will move and give me truth, peace, direction, and more. The goal is to make this the first thing I do instead of a last resort.

Consider a change. Looking into starting a new career? Sometimes our first career choice was a "practical" choice that met a need at that time, but it's not what you're passionate about. Not sure what you're passionate about? Spend time praying and meditating about it. What are you drawn to in your free time? Watching ER shows? Maybe it's a medical career. Going to the Humane Society? Maybe it's working with animals. Playing with children? Maybe you're called to be a teacher. It's a lot easier getting out of bed in the morning if we have work that gives us purpose.

Hormones. You knew this was coming. I'm all about the hormones. I'm kind of like a traveling salesman who won't leave your town. Ask your doctor to do a thorough blood test of your hormones and vitamin and mineral levels. If she won't, look for a different doctor. I did have to pay out of pocket a few hundred dollars since my insurance wouldn't cover it, but it was the best $300 I've ever spent. (Except for that time we had Mark's back waxed.)

"I CAN'T CHANGE THE DIRECTION OF THE WIND, BUT I CAN ADJUST MY SAILS TO ALWAYS REACH MY DESTINATION."
—JIMMY DEAN

IT'S A MARATHON, NOT A SPRINT.

Change didn't come for me overnight, but each day, each week was better, and it was only a matter of time before I began feeling like my old self again.

Give yourself small, attainable goals. Go to bed 15 minutes earlier each week until you fall into a natural rhythm, and turn off your phone at the same time. Walk three days a week for 15 minutes and add five minutes to each walk the following week, eventually building up to five days a week or more.

I urge you not to make exercise a chore. If it helps, don't do it alone. If you run with a friend, you have friend time and exercise time and outdoor time all at the same time. Talk about being productive!

Adjust goals as needed. I was going to do a triathlon with friends this July, but deadlines at work and other family issues kept me from getting in all of the needed training. Being the naturally calm person that I am, NOT, I began to freak out. Mark gave me the idea of doing it in a relay instead. So I decided to compete with my children (usually it's against them). Anastasia is the swimmer, I am the bicycle leg, and Noah is the runner. Now I'm excited about this, and it's a bonding time for me and my awesome kids. (Don't tell Mark, but our goal is to beat him. Maybe his back hair will slow him down.)

Breathe. Pray. Wait. The next right step is just around the corner.

"HEALING DOESN'T MEAN THE DAMAGE NEVER EXISTED. IT MEANS THE DAMAGE NO LONGER CONTROLS YOUR LIFE."
—AKSHAY DUBEY

Consider This:

- Emotional health is vital, and it's important that we don't hide or ignore it. There
  are others out there who, like me, are in
  the beginning stages of depression. If you
  don't address it now, you may fall deeper
  into the pit. Take an emotional inventory.
  How are you feeling? How do you feel in the
  morning when you wake up? Are you excited for the day? Do you feel down at night?
  Be honest with yourself.

- No one is immune to depression. We must
  be proactive in taking care of our minds
  and bodies. Be protective of your schedule so you don't wear out your mind and
  body. What steps are you taking to nurse
  and care for yourself? Are you spending
  time with friends? Are you making efforts to
  make friends? Are you getting enough quiet
  time? Do an emotional inventory.

CHAPTER 9
PHYSICAL HEALTH: AREN'T NIGHT SWEATS ENOUGH?

"ONLY REASON I'D TAKE UP JOGGING IS
SO I CAN HEAR HEAVY BREATHING AGAIN."
—ERMA BOMBECK

A big topic in health news lately is how sedentary we've become. As technology has developed, our need to move has diminished. It's only a matter of time before they develop a way for us to go to the bathroom and the refrigerator, simultaneously, without having to leave the couch, while watching TV. (For many us, walking to the bathroom and fridge are when we get most of our exercise!)

There are many benefits of physical activity, which I'm sure you already know. (But hey, we're getting older and forgetting more, so if I repeat myself, smile and nod and know I've already forgotten half of what I've written.) It's good conditioning for our cardiovascular system. It helps lower weight. It helps prevent diabetes. It aids our sleep and lubricates our joints. It flushes out the fog in our

brains and sends a glow to our skin via oxygen-rich blood. It builds muscle mass that protects our joints.

We can't play dumb anymore. They teach it to our kids in school. It's even on reality TV shows. We know physical activity is good for us, and we need to do it. For some it's a hobby, but for others, it's torture. There has to be a way to make it fun.

It wasn't a hobby for me, initially, but once I got started and over the hump (definition: state in where you no longer feel you are dying and realize that conquering the life ~~threatening~~ giving activity is actually fun), I enjoy it and look forward to it. The feel-good endorphins are pretty awesome.

I'm a yo-yo athlete. I don't mean that I compete and/or get an aerobic workout while playing with yo-yos. It means I have a tendency to go full force, slack off (usually during 90-degree temps or the holiday season(s)), and then go full force again, over and over and over. That being said, I have a *lot* of experience in getting started and restarted and restarted…

So, let's get started (in my case, restarted…again).

"I DON'T ALWAYS GO TO THE GYM. BUT WHEN I DO, I MAKE SURE EVERYONE ON FACEBOOK KNOWS ABOUT IT."
—UNKNOWN

PACE YOURSELF. DON'T LET OTHERS SET YOUR PACE, OR YOU MAY END UP NEEDING A PACEMAKER!

Remember, once you get started, don't beat yourself up if things don't always go perfectly. Sometimes life takes over, and we are not able to be at the fitness level we desire all the time. For example, I was on a good working-out streak and then this book deadline thing came up. Since I'm chronically distracted, I ended up needing to hide away in a house in the mountains and work around the clock. (Just between us, it was my plan all along to get some alone time, but don't tell Mark.)

Regardless, I have gotten a lot of work done, but have had very little exercise. I can fret over it, but I know I'm doing the best I can. I'm moving enough to defog my brain (which usually involves the bathroom or fridge). I may not be in a fitness-building phase, but at this moment, I'm maintaining, and that is better than nothing.

The key is baby steps. As we talked about before, start small. Do too much too soon and you risk getting injured. Going slower gives your muscles, joints, and connective tissues time to adapt to the many adventures you're about to take them on. Plus, it's less frustrating. If you wake up so sore the next day that you have to wait three days in order to work out again, it defeats the purpose.

"NEVER GO TO A DOCTOR WHOSE OFFICE PLANTS HAVE DIED."
—ERMA BOMBECK

TAKE A LOOK INSIDE. (DON'T WORRY. IT DOESN'T INVOLVE STIRRUPS!)

Okay, I'm repeating myself, but remember, we need repetition to help it stick. Go to the doctor, and get some blood work done. I can't tell you enough how much getting my hormones balanced has helped me. But hormones are not the only things with which doctors can help you.

I began my official "journey to 50" this past January, when I turned 49. I could tell something was not right internally, and one morning as I prayed, I asked God what I was supposed to do about my diet. I could tell certain foods didn't sit well, but I could never determine what was the culprit.

To make a short story long: A day after I prayed this, a friend who sells Arbonne products posted about going through a cleanse. I texted her asking for details. She wrote back sharing thoughts about their program, which consisted of us cutting out coffee (oh, Lord!), dairy (does that mean cheese?!), gluten (that wasn't too bad since my son has Celiac disease), sugar (chocolate doesn't have sugar in it...does it?!), soy (eh...), and alcohol (go ahead and shoot me!).

Besides that, you ate normal (if you could find any foods that didn't have these ingredients), used a few of Arbonne's products (protein powder, tea, energy packets, etc.)—all of which were incredible. (Don't worry, I don't sell the product, but I am a fan of it.)

It sounded like torture, similar to walking into church wearing a bikini after not shaving for three months. No one wants to be a part of that! But for some reason, I felt I was supposed to do it (the cleanse, not the bikini/no shave/church part). I mentioned this to Mark, hoping he'd say no, but to my surprise, he wanted to do it, too. *Dang it!*

Short story longer, we made it through the month. The first few days were hard, then it was easier, and by the end of the first week and a half, we were both feeling better than we ever have. Our moods were positive; our energy was strong. Mark lost 15 pounds at the end of the month. Me: five. SO not fair. Since it was basically dietary choices with whole food, we felt we should do it forever.

Only problem, it's hard to eat out or in the homes of others with this diet and, little by little, we went back to old habits.

Going through the cleanse helped me realize my diet really affected my energy and mood. I tried to narrow it down myself, but couldn't figure out which foods gave me these gut issues and foggy brain. I went back to the PA, and he ordered a blood panel that would give me an in-depth reading of food allergens. When the results came back, I was shocked.

I was extremely allergic to egg whites, black beans, and sunflower seeds. I was also allergic to avocados and almonds—not extreme, but to where I should not eat them more than every four days. I was eating all of the above throughout the day, *every* day, trying to be healthy.

What I was doing, in an attempt to be healthy, was aggravating my gut and making it hard on my body to absorb nutrients.

My point...go to the doctor if you are having any gut problems, and get their help in figuring this stuff out.

I have adjusted my diet, and I'm relearning how to feed myself, and it's going well. I'm mourning having to cut down on avocados and almonds. Breakfast has been hard. But my energy is continuing to improve, and when you have energy, it sure makes it easier to work out!

In grade school, I was often told, "You are what you eat." Health and PE teachers ingrained this in our brains. Now, dieticians and others in the health care field have discovered we aren't what we eat, we are what we absorb. If our bodies are not able to absorb the good nutrients we are taking in, due to inflammation or an allergy, then it's not aiding our health. This principle has helped me a great deal in fueling my body in a way that works for me.

"NO ONE IS LISTENING UNTIL YOU FART."
—UNKNOWN

IF YOUR GUT IS HAPPY, EVERYONE IS HAPPY.

Have you seen the comedy skit where the young man picks the girl up from her home, escorts her to the car, helps her into her seat, and shuts the door? As he walks around the back of the car, she lets one rip. He gets in the car and asks, "Have you already met Bobby and Sue?" She turns around and sees a couple giving her a knowing smile.

Even in my 50s, bathroom humor cracks me up. (Not sure why I just shared this.)

When I hear people speak of gut health, my first response is to think of Oma and Opa dealing with flatulence in their old age (Mom and Dad, I'm not speaking of you here! It's mainly Mark, but I'm hiding it under your names. Shhh…) A lot, if not all, of our health is tied to our gut. Get your gut healthy and other things fall in line.

As we just talked about, the gut is the second brain, and the brain is what moves the body. If your gut is happy, there's a good chance the rest of your body, *and those around you*, are happy as well.

If your gut is out of balance, it not only affects your digestion and absorption of your food, it can also affect your mood, thyroid, skin condition, and inflammatory issues, like rheumatoid arthritis and high blood pressure. If you want physical health, you need to begin internally. Research "leaky gut" online, and you'll open up a whole other world.

"EXERCISE IS INSPIRING...I LOVE TO BE SURROUNDED BY DUMB BELLS."
—UNKNOWN

WHICH IS MORE IMPORTANT, AEROBIC EXERCISE OR STRENGTH TRAINING?

Aerobic workouts are important as we age because they aid our heart health, balance our blood sugar, and help with brain function and memory. However, as we approach the age of 40, it's recommended that we put extra effort into strength training.

Strength training is good for other, less obvious reasons: it strengthens our bones and it helps with balance and agility. After the age of 40 (yikes, that was 10 years ago), we begin to lose 1 percent of our muscle mass every year. This can affect simple tasks such as getting out of the chair. If someone doesn't invent the gadget to help us potty and hit the fridge from the chair soon…hello, adult diapers!

But, we're still young. We're not lazy. We're strong and we're going to be proactive. Forty is the new 30, and we're going to do it differently. We're going to show the world that age is just a number that reminds us how much experience and wisdom we've obtained along the way. Don't let this get in your mind to break you down. Let's use it as motivation to get us up and moving.

So, how do we do it?

A friend of mine who works in the fitness industry said, as a general rule, if we're limited on time and have to choose—in our 30s the aerobic/strength ratio is 50/50 percent of our time. In our 40s it should be 60 percent strength and 40 percent aerobic. In our 50s it should be 70 percent strength and 30 percent aerobic and should remain here. Again, this is assuming you have a time constraint, but we don't have to worry about that because we have all the time in the world, and we're about to make fitness our hobby, right?!

Like with all exercise, begin wise and slow. Ten-15 minutes of strength training is a good start with lower weight and higher repetitions. If you're short on time, do upper body one day and lower body the next. Try to progress to 30-minute sessions, two-four times a week. You can use your body weight, free weights, dumbbells, barbells, resistance bands. Or attend classes at your local gym or hire a personal trainer if you need the accountability. Don't forget, there is always YouTube.

After a month or two, progress to heavier weights with lower reps for your strength training. For your aerobic workouts, add more intensity, focus on speed versus distance. New research is showing that intensity does more good in aging adults than longer workouts at a gradual pace or low weights. Just be sure to progress at a proper rate. Don't rush it.

"EXERCISE: A POOR MAN'S PLASTIC SURGERY."
—UNKNOWN

BE SURE TO RECOVER, AND DON'T FORGET TO SLEEP!

I need a new phrase besides, "as we age!" It sounds so depressing. How about "as we refine" or "as we mature" or "as we improve"? Regardless, this is not a bad thing. Our generation is kicking the butt of aging and not letting it sideline us. But there are adjustments that are needed.

Recovery is one of them. As we improve, we need more recovery time because we have so much awesomeness, we need more time to absorb it all. This is another reason why it is wise to workout with more intensity with longer rests in between. Joe Friel, author of the book, *Fast After 50,* is a big proponent of this method. I personally have been trying it, and I'm getting good results. Plus, it gives me more time to do other things, like sleep or spend time with my kids without the anxiety of, "I need to get another long workout in."

Recovery is also dietary. You need both carbohydrates and protein within 20 to 30 minutes after a workout. The jury is out on the ratio as it's constantly changing. I'm not a sports nutritionist, so I can't tell you what it is. The main goal is to get whole foods or a sports drink concoction. This can be either a sports recovery drink you can buy, or you can make your own in the form of a smoothie.

My favorite is to take a banana, a handful of frozen blueberries (for my brain health), some frozen strawberries, cover it with coconut milk (or almond milk), and add in a scoop of protein powder. If I have it on hand, I add in a small scoop of spirulina and a green veggie powder that I buy in the health section of the grocery store, and a handful of walnuts. Blend away and you have a tasty nutrient-dense recovery drink.

The goal is to get either your recovery food or drink in you as soon as possible to refuel muscles and energy storage. And, of course, rehydrate, regardless of the temperature. You still need water, even in cold temps. When you are dehydrated, your blood is thicker, causing your heart to work harder to pump the blood through your body. This puts unnecessary stress on the heart and fatigues you. So drink up!

"I REALLY THINK THAT TOSSING AND TURNING AT NIGHT SHOULD BE CONSIDERED EXERCISE!"
—UNKNOWN

HAVE FUN!

This is very important. Pick an activity that you enjoy and look forward to. Mix it up so you don't get bored and so you'll work a variety of muscle groups and avoid overuse injuries. We want to be in it for the long haul. If you enjoy it, chances are you will stick with it.

Let's get moving, laughing, and living and improve our overall health!

Consider This:

- Our bodies were created to move. Not only does our body get stronger, but our mood and disposition improve from exercise. Look at your environment and schedule. Where and how can you add more movement to your life? Can you take brisk walks during lunch? Squats by your desk? Toe raises as you brush your teeth? Stretch as you watch TV? Small and consistent steps will carry you farther than you realize.

- How is your internal health? Is your gut healthy? Look at what you are putting into your body. Maybe focus on one meal at a time. How can you improve your breakfast? Focus here and then move next to your lunch and then dinner.

- Remember, we're not what we eat, we're what we absorb. Does your gut gurgle after eating certain foods? Are you often bloated? If so, consider working with your doctor to see if you have any food allergies or sensitivities. By avoiding them, you'll feel better and your gut will be to better absorb the food you eat and better do its job.

SECTION 4

ORGANIC FAITH

Now we're gonna have us some church! Don't worry, I'm not going to preach. No one wants to hear that!

When I set out on my journey to 50, I was seeking health, whole health. I wanted every part of my being to be strong, clean, and well. It's hard for one to be healthy if we're sick in any area of our life. If your relationships are suffering, how can your emotional state be strong? If your body is sick, your mental health may suffer. We can't focus on some areas of our health and neglect others.

I believe a healthy spiritual life provides the foundation on which we build all of these. For me, I'm a person of faith. I believe in God, and for me, his name is Jesus. Have no fear, I will not try to convert you to my belief system in this section. However, I will share some principles that I find to be a common thread throughout all human life. For me personally, if my spiritual life suffers, everything suffers.

We'll talk of busyness, doubts, and the need and benefit of believing in ourselves.

I hope you will join me and continue reading. If delving into the spiritual side of things makes you nervous, jump over to the next section and maybe join us here another time.

"IF WE ARE TO GO FORWARD, WE MUST GO BACK AND REDISCOVER THOSE PRECIOUS VALUES—THAT ALL REALITY HINGES ON MORAL FOUNDATIONS AND THAT ALL REALITY HAS SPIRITUAL CONTROL."
—MARTIN LUTHER KING, JR.

CHAPTER 10
BUSYNESS: IT'S A MODERN-DAY PLAGUE

"ALL THE MISTAKES I EVER MADE IN MY LIFE WERE
WHEN I WANTED TO SAY NO, AND SAID YES."
—MOSS HART

What is busyness, anyway?

Busyness. It's a modern-day plague. It's highly contagious, and it's slowly killing us. It may not literally be killing us, though some would argue this is true. But it is sapping our joy, robbing our energy, and preventing us from truly living our life.

Some would argue with me. They love working around the clock. Their work and volunteer efforts revive them. They're passionate about them. To be clear, I'm not talking about workload or your job.

Busyness is the continual running around in a blur, bolting from one task to another, doing a lot, but accomplishing a little. You end the day with items crossed off your to-do list, which gives you a temporary sense of accomplishment, but it's not moving you toward your goal, your purpose, your calling. These tasks generally prevent you from doing "what you're supposed to be doing." You let the urgent take you from what's important.

Busyness is not a privilege, it's an obligation that makes you feel like you should be doing more, and if you're not, you're being wasteful and lazy. We're ashamed to talk about days off and are embarrassed if we only accomplish one item in a day.

I know I struggle with this. There are times I run into a friend and as we catch up, she'll ask, "So, what have you been up to lately?" If I don't have a long list of tasks to share with her, I feel guilty and start blubbering around, trying to make my "to-do" list sound bigger than it really is.

I've been working on this and have begun to own the right not to be busy all the time because by blubbering out a bogus to-do list, I'm passing on the germ of busyness to my friend.

"BUSYNESS IS A DRUG THAT A LOT OF PEOPLE ARE ADDICTED TO."
—UNKNOWN

HOW DID I CATCH THIS DISEASE?

"IT IS NOT ENOUGH TO BE BUSY; SO ARE THE ANTS. THE QUESTION IS: WHAT ARE WE BUSY ABOUT?"
—HENRY DAVID THOREAU

When I was in my 20s, it was hard to say "no" to volunteer opportunities, work, parties, trips, etc. because, one, I was single and on the prowl for Mr. Right. And, two, FOMO— the fear of missing out. If there was an adventure to be had, I wanted in and didn't want to miss anything. I needed excitement in my life because, in your 20s, nothing is scarier than being home on Friday night...alone.

Some may say our modern day culture brought on busyness. Technology has made it easier than ever before to do a lot of tasks at one time. We can bring work home and still be connected to colleagues. We can even take work on vacation with us.

The first five years of our company, Mark worked during every vacation. When he finally had a trip where there were no phone calls, texts, or emails, he returned a totally different man. He was revived and excited to get back to work. It sealed for us the importance of us, and our employees, having time off where they can leave work behind and be 100 percent present with their friends and families. In a small business, this is not always easy to do, but it's worth the effort.

It's not just technology. We're groomed from childhood to focus on performance. We're praised for our accomplishments and scorned if caught daydreaming. Believe me, I've been guilty for barking at Noah for hanging out inside his head instead of cleaning his room. Things do need to get done, but perhaps our busy, overbooked schedules are robbing our kids of time to get bored, sit, daydream, and create.

BUSYNESS DOES NOT EQUAL PRODUCTIVITY.

God created us to work. In Genesis 1:28, the second assignment He gave to Adam and Eve was to work and take care of the Earth and her creatures. The first was to have sex and multiply, but that is a whole other book. There is a God-given desire in each of us to work. We are either fulfilling it, avoiding it, or filling it with meaningless tasks taking us off course.

You can be busy doing *good* stuff, or even *God* stuff, but unless it's *your* stuff, the work you've been called to do, it's the *wrong* stuff.

When I was 27, I spent two years in southern Russia working with The Navigators. We were doing missions, working with World War II vets, orphans, the school system, etc. This was in the mid-1990s, not long after the Iron Curtain had fallen. The need was great and our time there was limited, so we seldom said "no" to any offer.

There were two older women on our team, Donna and Joanne, who were extremely wise. They adopted all of us single ladies (why do I hear Beyonce in my head right now?) and would invite us over, one at a time, and pour into our lives. One day, while I was visiting, they asked what I had been up to. I began sharing all that was going on, including some struggles I was dealing with. Joanne took a deep breath and said, "Laurie, there comes a time in your spiritual walk where you no longer struggle with certain sins. But if Satan can't get you bad, he'll get you busy."

At first I was a little offended by her comment. I wasn't sure what she was implying. Later at home, as I prayed through and processed her words, I saw the wisdom. I was so busy wearing myself out doing "good stuff" that I didn't even have the energy or time to figure out what God was asking of me. There are times that Satan lures us in, getting us so busy that we don't see God waving us over to an open door saying, "Yo! Over here! This is where I need you."

"THOSE WHO ARE WISE WON'T BE BUSY, AND THOSE WHO ARE TOO BUSY CAN'T BE WISE."

—LIN YUTANG

EFFECTS OF BUSYNESS.

At a glance, busyness seems harmless. As long as the majority is good stuff, we're doing okay. If we're strong, all we have to do is muscle through the fatigue, right?

Some are able to do so successfully, but when I try, I've found that prolonged bouts of busyness have these effects on me:

- I overreact. I shared this story in my book, *I Finally Love Him* (it's about God, not Mark), but it's such a good story, I'll share a condensed version here:

  Our son, Noah, had just been diagnosed with Celiac disease, meaning he could not eat gluten, anything with wheat, barley, or rye. Our house was filled with gluten, so the next few weeks we had to relearn how to cook and shop.

  Noah was a trooper, but he really missed certain foods. This was before the days of the gluten-free craze, and there were few options in the grocery store. He really loved quiche, so I researched how to make a gluten-free pie crust from scratch and worked on it for *hours,* literally, to get this stupid crust to stick together. I finally got it to work, put it in the oven, but this meant that dinner was running really late. "Don't snack, this is going to be worth it!"

  The timer rang. I opened the oven door and saw a perfectly baked quiche. It smelled so good. I reached in, pulled it out of the oven. As I backed up, I failed to see our 70-pound black lab lying on the floor behind me. I tripped. Up went the quiche and splattered all over the floor. "%$#@!* Louie!"

Louie is definitely not a smart dog, but he understood those words and fled for his life. The rest of the family heard my "French" and cautiously approached the kitchen and saw the quiche on the floor, "What happened?"

"Louie!"

"Ohhh." They all understood.

I reached in the utensil drawer, grabbed a fork, and said, "Get a fork. THIS is dinner!" I sat on the floor next to the pile of food and began eating. Anastasia, my mini me, immediately grabbed a fork and said, "Hmm...this looks good," and began to eat. (God knew I needed her.)

Mark and Noah held forks in their hands, leaned over and debated how to proceed. Mark stood up and said, "Nope. I see a dog hair. I can't do it. I'm going to Albertsons to get some fried chicken!"

"Great idea!"

We scooped up enough quiche for Noah, that was not polluted with floor nastiness or dog hair and the rest of us ate fried chicken. (Yes. I know baked chicken would have been better for us. But it couldn't be much worse than eating off my ~~dirty~~ kitchen floor.)

Our lives were in a stressful time as we were working to get my son healthy. He wasn't growing. He was often sick and his blood work showed him to be malnourished because of being Celiac. But I was still living my busy life, at the same time trying to learn to cook for and take care of Noah.

Keep in mind I was hangry, but my outburst made him feel guilty. He later shared that he felt his disease kept the rest of us from being able to go out to eat (this was before most restaurants had gluten-free options) and that he was causing me more work.

I adore Noah and would sacrifice anything for him. *He* needed to be my priority, not my busyness. It was a good wake up call to slow down and focus on what was *important*—helping my son learn to live with his new normal.

- I neglect my calling. This piggybacks off of my first point, and we've talked briefly about this already. But there are daily "callings" that God is asking of us. They are what I like to call "divine interruptions." It may be a neighbor who needs a meal, a friend going through a divorce who really needs a shoulder to cry on, an elderly neighbor who needs a ride to an appointment, a lonely couple, new to the area, who could really use an invite for dinner.

  It's tempting to see these as interruptions, but in reality, they are God divinely orchestrating, asking, choosing you to help His children. It's a blessing to be a blessing. I wonder how many I've missed out on because I was too busy to notice.

- I miss the beauty of rest. As I mentioned, our daughter, Anastasia, takes cello lessons. In her old school, they didn't offer orchestra like they do at her present school. She's spent the past four months taking lessons in hopes of learning enough to be in the orchestra next year. She's been working hard and has made a lot of progress.

  At a recent lesson, she was playing a piece for Micah, her teacher, but was not fully holding the rests—the breaks written into the music. Instead, she was half pausing in order to get to the next notes more quickly. In her eyes, if she wasn't playing the notes, she wasn't making music.

  He stopped her and explained how composers strategically write "rests" in the music in order for those listening (and playing) to absorb what they had just heard.

  "They are sacred moments of silence, so our minds can process the beauty of the music and then be ready to receive, or give, more."

  He played the piece for us with the proper rests, and it was beautiful. Instead of feeling rushed, it felt right. It was medicine for my soul. I almost cried.

  It was a big "aha!" moment for me, and I immediately texted myself notes before I lost his words. Probably not the reaction he was looking for—play beautiful music and then watch the mom pick up her phone and begin texting. (Note to self...apologize to Micah.)

IS THERE A DIFFERENCE BETWEEN REST AND LAZINESS?

"NEVER BE SO BUSY AS NOT TO THINK OF OTHERS."
—MOTHER TERESA

God created us to work, but in the Ten Commandments, He spends a great deal of time telling us to take a Sabbath and rest. I love this about Him. I love rest, but in a culture addicted to comfort and leisure, there is a fine line between having rest and being lazy.

Once again, I hit social media and asked people to help me define the difference between rest/being still and laziness. A friend, who is a widower, shared, "I'm borrowing this heavily from Paul Tillich. I would make it analogous to loneliness and solitude. Loneliness expresses the pain of isolation where solitude expresses the joy of it. Laziness is not engaging in life where stillness celebrates life by observing."

I loved that. As a fairly new widower, his words spoke real-life experience.

Another shared, "Rest involves contemplation. Being lazy usually involves potato chips and trash TV."

Been there. Done that!

There's a huge difference between rest and laziness.

In rest, to twist the beautiful words of Anastasia's cello teacher, you're pausing to absorb the moments you just lived. You're processing, analyzing, or just plain taking a break in order to recover from the chaos.

In laziness, you're avoiding responsibility. You're putting off the needs of others. You're running from reality because it's painful and takes work.

The peace of God cannot hit a moving target. Be still. Pray. Meditate. Say "no" more often unless you truly feel called to say "yes." Take a true Sabbath weekly.

Your worth is not found in what you do. It's found in who you are. It's hard to know who you are if you're too busy to get to know her.

Rest is of God. Enjoy it.

"BEWARE THE BARRENNESS OF A BUSY LIFE." —SOCRATES

Consider This:

- Have you caught the busyness bug? Do you have trouble saying "no" when asked to take on a task? Are you constantly running around from one activity to another? Does your mind constantly play through your "to-do" list? Do you have trouble turning your mind off at night? Are you able to enjoy the present moment, or are you thinking about what's next on your list? Work is good. We were created to work, but we weren't asked to do it all. If you answered "yes" to two or more of these questions, maybe it's time to slow down and cut some stuff out.

- Do you take time to rest, or do you feel guilty taking time off? Rest is vital. We need it in order to recuperate, in order to come back stronger. Do not let guilt rob you of the blessing of rest.

Psalms

CHAPTER 11
QUESTIONS: I HAVE SO MANY DOUBTS

> "TO DOUBT EVERYTHING OR TO BELIEVE EVERYTHING ARE TWO EQUALLY CONVENIENT SOLUTIONS; BOTH DISPENSE WITH THE NECESSITY OF REFLECTION."
> —HENRI POINCARÉ

Doubt is often a word with negative connotations. When Mark doubts something I've said, I'll automatically assume he either doesn't believe me and/or is trying to prove me wrong. *"It's true. Abby and I did invite Charlie Sheen and Emilio Estevez to church with us!"* But this is untrue. (The part about doubt. We really did invite the brothers to church, but they turned us down.) It's an uncertainty, an indecision of what you believe. Left undone and without reflection, little will change unless another intervenes and somehow persuades you to their line of thinking.

I'm a slow learner, and I don't like to be persuaded. I prefer more to learn by experience, especially when it comes to my spiritual life.

Doubt in your spiritual walk is not necessarily a sign of weakness. It doesn't reveal a lack of faith. It doesn't mean you don't have faith. When Jesus prayed in the garden, before His crucifixion, He had doubt and asked God if there was another way around it.

But the key here is that He was praying. He was honestly seeking God to know the truth, and He got His answer. We can, too, as long as we're truly seeking to know the truth.

"WHEN IN DOUBT, PUNT!"
—JOHN HEISMAN

MY STORY OF DOUBTING GOD.

I grew up in the church. It was a wonderful community of people who helped raise me and my sister and brother. It was a second family for us. But I wasn't quite as angelic as my sister and brother. I loved the people in the church, I just didn't like going to church.

I believed in God. I believed the stories they taught me in Sunday school. But I also believed in Santa Claus and the Easter Bunny, and they were eventually taken away from me. Did I believe because it was my culture? Did I believe because I needed someone to believe in? I wasn't sure.

College came, and it tested my belief system. I partied hard. The only times I prayed was right before tests or at night while sneaking into my parent's home, hoping I wouldn't wake my mother. I still had belief in God, just not much need for God. (Well, I needed a lot of help with those tests.)

A couple years down the road, the partying lifestyle was wearing. Some friends and I went dancing one night and had a horrible time. The guys were crude and the music was trashy. Frustrated, we left. On the ride home, I looked out the window with a pit in my stomach, when my friend said, "There has to be more to life than this!"

She articulated exactly what I was feeling.

The next day she called me, "You're not going to believe what I just did. I went to church, and it was awesome. They have a great singles group, and the guys are SO hot!"

That was all I needed to hear. We began attending that church in search of good men. We didn't find the men, but we both found God. I spent years in this church, learning more about God and developing a true relationship with Him.

Flash forward six years, Mark and I are married, and had been living in Santiago, Chile, with our son, Noah, who was three months old at the time. We had been there for about a year and a half, working as missionaries. Yep, bet you didn't see that one coming. I sure didn't either. Last thing I thought I'd ever be was a missionary, or an author. (I hated writing papers in school!) God has a sense of humor.

Some of the other missionary women and I decided to do a Bible study together. We were all very busy working and serving others, but were feeling a dryness in our own spiritual lives.

I loved it at first. It was great to be with like-minded women and have a break from the struggle of trying to learn Spanish. I enjoyed the study in the beginning. But, after a while, it was wearing on me. It was a study where we did homework lessons during the week and once a week, we'd meet at someone's home, go over the homework, and then watch a video of the author with more teaching.

Each week I'd get behind in the lessons due to new mommy duties. I'd feel overwhelmed as I rushed to catch up.

One day, as I was scurrying to get my homework done, every word the author had written irked me. She kept talking about how much she *loved* the Lord, and how much she *loved* His Word. It was driving me crazy.

Why was it bothering me? Everything she said was beautiful and true. It wasn't her personally. I've always enjoyed her work. It was something else.

Thinking on this, I then wondered, when was the last time I talked about how much I loved God? I couldn't remember. When was the last time I said "I love God"? I couldn't remember that either.

Do I love God?

What does it mean to love God?

I don't think I love God!

I don't. I don't love God!

A rush of dread and fear washed over me. Everything I had just thought felt like the truth. What did this mean? Was I walking away from my faith? Did I not believe in God anymore? How would this affect my family? Would we lose our jobs as missionaries? I may be wrong, but I don't think there are too many agencies out there that want to hire missionaries who are doubting their love for God.

Noah began to cry and my thoughts were lost in the moment. I'm the queen of putting things on the back burner (probably because of busyness ☺), and I went on with my day.

"SEEDS OF FAITH ARE ALWAYS WITHIN US; SOMETIMES IT TAKES A CRISIS TO NOURISH AND ENCOURAGE THEIR GROWTH."
—SUSAN L. TAYLOR

THE STORY
GETS OUT.

"DOUBT IS AN INCENTIVE TO TRUTH, AND PATIENT INQUIRY LEADETH THE WAY."
—HOSEA BALLOU

Later that day, we met at the house of my friend who was hosting the Bible study. I sat on the floor with Noah next to me in his carrier. We began the study, going over our homework. I had not thought any more about my questioning of my love for God until we came to the same section in the study.

My heart began pounding, and I felt winded, as if I had just done a 50-yard sprint (okay, 25-yard sprint). What was going on? Did God want me to share my doubts with this group? I sure hoped not. These feelings were all so new to me, I wasn't sure if I was ready. We were a talkative group, so I knew my next hurdle would be finding a moment of silence for me to interject. I didn't want to be rude and interrupt, so I figured I was safe.

Right at that moment, there was silence. That awkward silence where everyone is looking around, not sure what to say. *Dang it!*

I began talking, mostly gibberish. I don't really remember what I was saying, but as I talked, the women were all smiling and nodding their heads. This was an incredible group of women. I loved them all. They were like family, and I was safe with them. So then I said...

"I don't think I love God anymore!"

Drop the mic, walk out of the room...crickets.

To find out what happened after that you have to read my book, *I Finally Love Him.* Bahahaha. Just kidding. Bad joke. But, it does tell the story of my journey to rediscover my love for God. (I have a fixation with journeys, eh?! I blame Mark and Alaska.)

The gist of what happened is that these women were supportive, but no one knew what to do with me. Missionaries don't usually go around telling people they no longer love God. It was a first for all of them, I'm sure. One of the ladies in the group told me, "Of course, you love God. You're just going through a rough patch right now. You have a new baby. You're in a foreign country. It will get better in time."

Everything she said was true, and I wanted to believe these points were the root cause of my doubts. But inside I knew it was more. It was deeper than my circumstances. I felt as if God was telling me not to excuse this away. Don't hide behind my doubts, but instead bring them to Him, and He'd help me work through them.

So, I did.

One by one, various doubts would arise—about God, natural disasters, disease, poverty. Did God even love me personally? There are so many of us here on earth. How can He love each of us?

As I tackled each doubt, God would reveal hindrances unique to my life that were blocking me from fully experiencing Him. Some of it was hard, for it brought up past hurt. Some of it was common to many. All of it important, for during this time of doubt, my faith was no longer taught to me by my family, it had become my own.

Today, I still have doubts, but they are not about my relationship with God. When a new topic of doubt arises,

I don't hide it in the back of my heart. I take it to God. He always shows up. Sometimes I just have to be patient.

"FAITH IS THE REFUSAL TO PANIC."
—DAVID MARTYN LLOYD-JONES

Our doubts are nothing we should shy away from, for they may merely be God shaking our foundations in order to wake us up, jolting us out of the routines that distract and blind us from seeing and engaging with Him. He's a God who wants to be known.

God is so big, we can't expect to see all of Him or know all of Him at once. We take our doubts before Him, truly seeking Him, and it is in these moments He will reveal more of Himself to us. When we are mature enough in our faith to have the strength to question Him, He knows we are ready to see and receive more of Him. The problem with many of us today is we're satisfied with just knowing a little of Him. But, oh, He's so much more.

We just have to ask to see it and wait.

"DOUBT ISN'T THE OPPOSITE OF FAITH; IT IS AN ELEMENT OF FAITH."
—PAUL TILLICH

Consider This:

- Do a spiritual inventory. Are you at peace, or are you anxious? Are you growing in your spiritual life, or are you going through the motions? Was there a time in your life you felt closer to God? What do you think about the most during the day? How do you begin and end your days? Are you taking time to have focused prayer or meditation? If my spiritual life is off, then everything is off. Take at least five minutes each day to pray, breathe, and quiet your mind before God. It will do wonders.

- Do you have doubts in your belief system? Don't be afraid to question God. Ask Him to reveal truth to you. No question is too big or small, but it will eat away at you if you don't address it.

CHAPTER 12:
BELIEVE: THE GLUE THAT KEEPS ME FROM FALLING APART

"TO BE A CHAMP, YOU HAVE TO BELIEVE IN
YOURSELF WHEN NOBODY ELSE WILL."
—SUGAR RAY ROBINSON

The doubt we just talked about can be a productive tool, as long as we are actually seeking truth. However, there is another doubt that is poisonous and paralyzing. It is doubt in ourselves.

We all have been entrusted with gifts that we are to share with the world. The No. 1 weapon used against us is not believing in ourselves. We have to trust and believe that we're good enough. A woman walking in God's strength can do anything. We just have to believe and do the work.

"MANY OF LIFE'S FAILURES ARE PEOPLE WHO DID NOT REALIZE HOW CLOSE THEY WERE TO SUCCESS WHEN THEY GAVE UP."
—THOMAS EDISON

The Bible is full of stories of God calling and entrusting people with assignments. The reaction to these callings varied.

Some accepted it right away. When Gabriel told Mary that God had chosen her to become the mother of Jesus, she asked one simple question, "You know I'm a virgin, right?" (I took the liberty of paraphrasing here.) She, then, was like, "Sure. Whatever God wants," and proceeded to give this eloquent prayer that was way beyond her years and nothing close to anything I've ever heard come out of a teenager's mouth.

She believed and went on to have the honor of being closer to and knowing Jesus on a different level than anyone else on Earth.

Some argued it away. God asked Moses to return to Egypt because He wanted to use him to help free the Israelites from Egyptian slavery. Moses immediately looked at his personal flaws, "Have you hearr, hearrrdd mmm me speak?! Ain't nooobbody will lisssten tooo mm mmee!" He continued to argue with God, asking Him to choose someone else. In frustration, God finally agreed to have Moses' brother, Aaron, go and be the mouth of this leadership team.

He believed in God, but not in himself.

Some mostly believed, were tested, and fled, only to return stronger. The disciples had a front-row seat and saw the many works of Jesus. They also heard His teaching and had a true friendship with Him. However, when Jesus was arrested and crucified on the cross, they either fled and hid, watched from afar and denied Him, or witnessed the crucifixion but didn't fight for Him. However, once He rose from the dead and appeared to them, everything changed.

Their belief in God was so strong, it overshadowed all their insecurities and fears. They mobilized and changed the world.

As humans, it's hard for us to perfectly believe, especially in ourselves. We know all of the nastiness that lurks in our hearts. The doubt that floods our minds. The insecurity that locks our mouths. The fear that paralyzes our feet.

I am a woman full of flaws, and those flaws have a way of blurring my vision and preventing me from seeing the potential that lies within me, if only I believed.

Proverbs 29:18 says, "Where there is not vision, the people perish." (KJV)

We were created with a purpose, and when we don't see it and fulfill it, something inside of us dies. Jesus promised us in John 14:12 that as long we are following His guidance, we'd be able to do even greater things than He did on Earth.

"I tell you the truth, anyone who believes in me will do the same works I have done, and even greater works, because I am going to be with the Father." (NLT)

So, if you feel led to open a bakery, take in foster children in your home, or start that non-profit, what's keeping you from doing it? You may not have all the skill sets needed, but that is why we work in teams. Look around you. Who can you team up with? Pray for them, and those who can help will slowly emerge at the right time.

"IF WE ALL DID THE THINGS WE ARE CAPABLE OF DOING, WE WOULD LITERALLY ASTOUND OURSELVES."
—THOMAS EDISON

When starting our company, it amazed me how people we needed would appear at the right time: editor, investor, mentor, employees with different skill sets. It all fell into place. It hasn't always been easy, but that doesn't mean we're supposed to quit either. It's so tempting to throw in the towel in our darkest hour, but so often, if we hold out just a little bit longer, we see we were just minutes from entering the light. And I'm not talking about the light at the end of the tunnel. I'm talking about seeing your dream become a reality.

VOICES
BATTLING
INSIDE MY
HEAD.

Initial belief is easy for me. I'm the type who comes up with an idea and immediately believes I can do it. But it doesn't take long for the two voices inside of my head to begin to battle. The first voice is giving me all the reasons I cannot do it. All my inadequacies. The lack of funds. The lack of time. My lack of ability. On and on they go, louder and louder, as long as I fuel them with my attention. It's only a matter of time before I convince myself that the idea is foolishness.

The second is a voice that cheers me on with words of encouragement. This is your strength. You were made for this. You can fill this need. This person can help you here. You have been chosen for this task.

This voice doesn't always yell. It also whispers because, in order for me to hear it, I need to give my full attention and listen. It is often here where wisdom is found. Following wisdom doesn't always make sense and can be hard to explain to others.

Here's an illustration of a time when my brother and sister-in-law listened to the whisper:

We've lived in Boise for eight years now. All of my side of the family still lives on the east coast, so usually my family will fly east and visit them for the holidays due to logistics. However, they've all wanted to visit Boise, so one by one most all have headed west to visit us, except for my younger brother and his family. Due to his job, it never worked out.

This past year, the calendars finally matched. He and his family were going to drive my parents out so my parents could have a long visit with us. Brian and his family would visit for a week and then fly home to Virginia. He found one-way tickets for his whole family. He bought them, and everything was set for them to come visit us in June. I was giddy and began making preparations for their visit, and then I got the call.

"I know you're going to think I'm weird, but, for some reason, Sarah and I feel I'm supposed to come visit you right away, alone. Like within three weeks. But, instead of visiting you a week, it would only be for three days." *Three days!*

Yeah, I did think it was weird at first, and I was bummed because I wanted time with Sarah and my nieces as well. Plus, my week-long visit with my brother was now cut down to three days. I tried to act like a big girl and got on board with the new plan.

Wouldn't you know, a night before he arrives, Mark gets sick with full-blown flu (and he's not the easiest patient). In my head, I'm wondering if Brian's change of plans was a good idea after all. (And I'm praying Brian doesn't catch the bug and get sick on the plane.)

So the first half of my first day with Brian is spent caring for Mark. Eventually, Mark falls asleep so Brian and I take off, and I show him parts of Boise. Over the three days, we spent hours in coffee shops and ate long, leisurely lunches while the kids were at school. At night, he and I'd play board games with the kids and talk as Mark rested on the couch.

The three days I had with Brian were awesome. It was quality time with my little brother that I haven't had since I was in my late 20s. It was a treasure. It was perfect!

The next month, my mom had her heart attack and stroke, and it then became very clear why God changed the dates of Brian's visit. He wasn't robbing us of having a week together. He was rearranging the dates in order for us to still have quality time together before life got crazy.

Brian and Sarah were in tune with God's voice in their heads. It wasn't a yell, but it was very clear what they were to do. They heard it and believed it and acted on it. Because they did, I was blessed to have that time with him.

"IF YOU HEAR A VOICE WITHIN YOU SAY 'YOU CANNOT PAINT,' THEN BY ALL MEANS PAINT, AND THAT VOICE WILL BE SILENCED."
—VINCENT VAN GOGH

If I'm going to step out and take that leap of faith, I need to be able to believe, not just in God, but myself. Sometimes it's easier to believe and trust in God. The struggle is believing and trusting in yourself.

"IT IS NEVER TOO LATE TO BE WHAT YOU MIGHT HAVE BEEN."
—GEORGE ELIOT

HOW DO YOU DECIPHER BETWEEN THE MANY VOICES AND KNOW WHICH ONE TO FOLLOW?

We all have big dreams and goals inside of us. Some are realistic, others—not so much. (Yeah, I finally gave up my dream of being an Olympian. I could never decide which sport to compete in, otherwise, I probably could have made it to Rio. Oh, well.) Many of these dreams remain hidden inside us not just because we don't believe in ourselves, but because we wonder if it's even a dream worth pursuing, especially if our actions could affect those we love (e.g., less pay, job insecurity, more time traveling).

Here are some guidelines I've found to be useful:

- Is it a dream that won't die? Does it keep popping up in your conversations? Do you catch yourself thinking about it repeatedly when you're alone? Has it been with you over time? God-given dreams don't die. If you ignore them long enough, you may miss your opportunity or have to do it on a smaller scale. But if it's engraved on your heart, it won't leave you.

- Does it give you life, or does it drain you? Are you energized when you think about it? Do you want to talk about it with everyone? Do you want to read about it, learn about it, watch movies or documentaries on it? Start with baby steps. Apply for a business license. Get the paperwork on becoming a foster parent. Buy a pair of running shoes and a book on marathons. Apply for a 501(c)(3). Get your passport, and buy a book on your destination of choice. How do you feel afterwards? Does it fuel your dream, or does it drain it?

- Does it take you out of your comfort zone? Great things seldom happen in the comfort zone. Take a baby step out of the boat. Put your foot in the water. Allow yourself to see you are braver and stronger than you believe. Are you willing to try? If you want to change yourself and your life, you can't remain in the boat. Trust God, and trust yourself. You'll be amazed at what happens next.

- Does it harm others? Will it hurt another or harm their reputation? God never asks us to hurt others. Keep in mind, small sacrifices are not always bad. Cutting back on luxuries or having to work longer hours (temporarily) are small sacrifices that are often needed when beginning a new adventure. If you want to run a marathon, you'll have less time for TV. If you want to start a non-profit, you may not be able to afford the pricey coffee. If you want to travel the world, you may need to sell your car. The sacrifices will seem so small when you are living your dream.

- Does it honor God? This is a filter you must take everything through. If your dream does honor God, the sky is the limit. If it doesn't conflict with His Word and His desire for you, then go for it and hold on. You are about to fly. Just be prepared. There will be turbulence that may shake you up. But keep moving forward, and you will eventually reach your destination.

Jesus said He came to give us a full and abundant life (John 10:10). It honors Him when we fully live. The Bible also tells us that God gave us everything for our enjoyment (1 Tim. 6:17). He wants us to pursue our goals. He wants us to be happy, do work that excites us, take trips that refuel us, and make goals that expand us.

Believe. Believe it's possible. Believe you are capable. Believe God will enable you.

There is a lot of scary stuff happening in our world today. It's tempting to put on our sweats, hide inside our homes, and be safe. Don't turn your back on life. Work hard, play hard, pray like crazy, and believe, believe, believe!

"EVEN IF I KNEW THAT TOMORROW THE WORLD WOULD GO TO PIECES; I WOULD STILL PLANT MY APPLE TREE."
—MARTIN LUTHER

Consider This:

- Is there a yearning inside of you, an unfulfilled desire that has not died over the years? Have you taken any steps to accomplish it? If not, why? What is keeping you from believing you are capable? What voice are you listening to? Don't let the doubts in your head keep you from moving forward. Believe in yourself. You can do it.

- Take the time to do an analysis of your dream. If it gives you life, helps others, honors God, takes you out of your comfort zone, and more, then go for it. Pray like crazy, and take that first step. There will be ups and downs, but the reward and sense of accomplishment will be so worth it.

"THE VERY ACT OF BELIEVING CREATES STRENGTH OF ITS OWN."
—UNKNOWN

SECTION
5

OUTRAGEOUS FUN

To me, nothing is more therapeutic than a good belly laugh. I can be stressed out of my brains, but if someone makes me laugh, I can feel the tension melting out of my body. It's a survival mechanism we've been given to help endure the craziness of this world. If only we could bottle it up and have it on hand at all times. We wouldn't have to worry about being addicted to it, either.

Wherever there is laughter, people are having fun (unless it's at the expense of someone else, of course).

Ask a person, "What do you want out of life?" and you will get a variety of answers. A wife may say, "To love and be loved." But a husband may say, "To be served and be served...a lot." Ha! Just kidding...sort of.

For a career woman, it may be attaining a certain level in her company.

For an artist, it may be to create a masterpiece that brings joy to others.

For a nurse, it may be to comfort and help heal the sick.

For a teacher, it may be to guide and train the children of our future.

For a musician, it may be to compose a song that gives peace.

For a mom, it may be to raise her children into healthy and thriving adults who will make the world a better place.

We may all want different things out of life, but there's a common thread within all of us, one thing we all want— fun! We want to do our "thing" and have a good time doing it.

If we don't live our lives with intention, the world can drain us and suck us into its whirlwind. That may be fun for a little bit, but if we don't take back control of our lives, it leaves us nauseated and dizzy with no clear direction.

So, I'm turning 50. Nothing like a big birthday to slap me in the face and remind me to quit wasting my time and truly live. We all have been given a limited amount of days (sounds morbid, but it's true). We need to make sure we're not wasting them on things that drain us and that we're living intentionally to fulfill the desires of our hearts.

CHAPTER 13
ENERGY: PLUG THE DRAIN

"YOUR OPTIMISM TODAY WILL DETERMINE YOUR LEVEL OF SUCCESS TOMORROW."
—JON GORDON

When I was young(er), time went by soooo slowly. It felt like eternity for Christmas to arrive, and that was on Christmas Eve! Now, time is flying. It seems like just yesterday was my 49th birthday. My sister-in-law emailed me today, saying that it was my half birthday, and that she'd love to take me out to celebrate it. Which means, by the time you are reading this book, I will have already turned 50, and dang, that *sounds* old!

There's a chance people will start respecting me more in my 50s. Nah…who am I kidding?

Here's the thing, I don't feel it, and I'm actually excited about turning 50. I don't see it as a bad thing. I'm ready to celebrate because Mama may be getting older, but she's feeling better and better each day. I thought turning half-a-century old would be depressing, but I'm ready to celebrate it, and I think a lot of it has to do with the healthier view on aging. People are not letting age slow them down.

But you have to be intentional in how you manage each day, each decision. Otherwise, before you know it, you're living a life that someone else has authored for you, leaving you tired, unfulfilled, and with bad hips.

"I WANT TO LIVE A LIFE THAT I WOULD WANT TO TAKE NOTES ON."
—BOB GOFF

PLUG THE
HOLES IN
YOUR BUCKET
SO YOU DON'T
RUN DRY.

One of the reasons I feel better this year is because I've plugged a lot of holes in my bucket that were draining my energy. Some were big. Some were small. Others barely visible, but they all were sucking me dry.

These were not leaks of me pouring into someone else's life. Nope. It was wasted water, pooling in the corner, collecting mildew, making puddles that my crazy dog lies in and then comes into the house on my clean floor kind of leaks. Wasted water that is helping no one (except the crazy dog).

We all have them. They are like dripping faucets. (I'm just all over the water metaphors!) Drip. Drip. Drip. Slowly etching into your margins, your free time, your quietness, your peace. Before you know it, you're just one drip away from blowing that blood vessel that pops out on your forehead when you are mad.

Where is the joy and fun in that?

If we are to have an abundant life full of joy, purpose, laughter, accomplishments, fulfilling dreams, loving others, serving the poor, helping the sick, traveling the world, skiing that mountain, feeding the hungry, or hanging with our kids, we're going to need a lot of energy, and we can't afford to waste any of it.

If there is an area in your life that is draining you, if possible, consider doing what you can to seal that sucker and get about your business.

"YOU ONLY HAVE SO MUCH ENERGY FOR EACH DAY. DON'T FIGHT BATTLES THAT DON'T MATTER."
—JOEL OSTEEN

WHERE DO WE START?

"THE SECRET OF GETTING AHEAD IS GETTING STARTED."
—MARK TWAIN

First thing we need to do is identify areas of our lives that are draining us. It could be a snarky boss that steals all of your ideas and claims them as her own. It could be a job that no longer challenges or inspires you. You walk into the office each day and immediately begin to count the hours. It could be an abusive relationship, either physical or emotional. Perhaps your partner controls you with their lies and sucks any freedom and independence out of you. It could be a needy friendship that is one-sided. All they do is take but give nothing back to you in return. It can be an organization you volunteer for that takes you for granted, pouring jobs on you that no one else wants.

Take an analysis of your life. Are there certain areas or people you dread? Do they cause anxiety or fear or depressive emotions?

Once you identify them, see if and where you can make changes. It may be as simple as talking with your boss and seeing if there are other job opportunities within your company.

Talk with your egocentric friend. Perhaps she was not aware of her needy ways, but now that you've mentioned it, she sees it and will be more considerate.

When Mark and I started the business, it was just Mark and me, along with some people we contracted out, until we were able to bring them on full-time. I enjoyed it during that time as the group of us tried to figure it out together. You name it, I did it. I built furniture. I looked for office space. I figured out the mailing system. I helped with cover designs. I even did some editing, which was the scariest part.

We were a mom and pop shop and I loved working with "Pop."

We've grown a lot over the years and brought in a lot more people as we became a real business. Jobs I used to do are now covered by people who are actually gifted in that area. (Seriously if only; You, new: how badly my grammer is!> What where we thinking have me edit?!)

I worked in the office full-time, but each day I walked into the office, I dreaded it. I loved the social side of it. I loved being with our peeps, they're awesome and fun, but the work I was doing did not fulfill me. Each meeting I attended, I felt defeated. I am *not* a business person. Working on the business side of the company depleted my creative side so much there was a period that I eventually stopped writing.

A while back, we ran out of space in our office before our contract was up. I volunteered to work from home during this time, and the minute I left the office, life began to return to me. I knew then it was the right decision. I'm still part of the company. Mark and I still talk business at home...ALL the time. I still go in for the occasional meeting. But my energy and time are now focused on creating content and helping others do the same. And I'm so happy! I feel like I have my lifeline again.

I'm not saying that you should do only what you enjoy. There are still tasks and jobs I have to do, but that's life. My point is to find work that energizes and gives you joy, at least most of the time. Test your options. If there is a change that can be made, think it over, test it. It may be the best decision you ever make.

"YOU CAN ONLY BECOME TRULY ACCOMPLISHED AT SOMETHING YOU LOVE. DON'T MAKE MONEY YOUR GOAL. INSTEAD PURSUE THE THINGS YOU LOVE DOING AND THEN DO THEM SO WELL THAT PEOPLE CAN'T TAKE THEIR EYES OFF OF YOU."

—MAYA ANGELOU

What if we can't change it? There will be areas in our lives that we can't change, and it's unfortunate. I shared a Maya Angelou quote in the beginning of the book, and I think it's worthy of repeating, "If you don't like something, change it. If you can't change it, change your attitude." I find this to be the key to most things in life. We won't always be able to fit things into the "perfect" mold. But the one thing we do have control over is our attitude. And attitude is everything.

Employment. If you can't change out your snarky boss who keeps stealing your ideas and claiming them as her own, instead of allowing her to have power over you, try seeing her through compassionate eyes. (I know, not always easy!) See her as the insecure girl who needs the attention. Often when I learn peoples' backstories, it gives me more compassion for them, and I'm able to overlook, maybe handle, any disrespect they cause me. Again, not always easy to do.

Maybe it's a co-worker who is wearing you down with negativity. Try seeing them through a different lens as well. If it goes on too long, ask for a transfer or a change in schedule. Try to see the human side of everyone. We live in a world filled with a lot of broken and hurt people. If you can be one of the ones to help put them back together again, you're doing the world a service.

Parenting. It could be you're in a difficult phase of parenting, a colicky baby, a rebellious teenager. As much as you'd like, you have no control over your situation—and you can't return them for a replacement. They are our jewels. What has helped me during these periods is reminding myself this is usually a phase and it, too, will pass. The most important thing is that they know we love them unconditionally. We may not be able to condone adolescent behavior. There may be consequences, but with a lot of prayer and patience, in time it will pass and, hopefully, we will all survive it (and still be sane). I was once that child. I put so many gray hairs on my parents' heads in my teens and college years. But we all made it. There's hope somewhere deep in that.

Marriage. This is a sensitive one. I'm not speaking here of anyone in an abusive relationship. Your situation is completely different. I'm praying for you now and hope my words do not hurt you. You are precious, beautiful, and worthy of so much more! Please get help and know I will continue to pray for you.

I am speaking of marriage where two people have grown apart, are negligent of one another, and possibly on the verge of making a bad mistake. Don't do it! Give it another chance, especially if your issues come from boredom or stress. Please forgive me if I'm overstepping my boundary. If you have kids, give it more time for their sake.

Don't look at how your partner has changed over the years—search yourself. Have you changed? Did you used to be more encouraging? Did you speak to him in a more loving tone? Did you serve him more? Did you talk well of him to others? Did you compliment him? Did you compliment him in front of others? Did you used to cuddle more? Did you use to send him "special" text messages? Did you leave love notes in his suitcase when he traveled? (Just so you know, this is convicting the crap out of me right now!)

If you answered "yes," try doing these again. Don't expect change from him overnight. Give it time. There may be thick walls that have been built up between you over the years. It may take some time to bring them down. But focus on how YOU have changed, and begin there. Excuse me for a second, I need to go send a "special" text!

Look in the mirror. This piggybacks off my point above. Do a self-assessment. Do you have bad attitudes, habits, vices that may be doing you physical or emotional harm? Guilt and shame run deep and hide behind many masks. Many of these are hard for us to change, and they eat away at our self-worth, which is very draining. Some, with time and awareness, we can conquer alone. Others, we need the help of family, friends, or a professional. If this is the case, I urge you to seek out help. These can drain so many areas of your life. If left untouched, in time, it can implode. You are worth so much more than this! Do not doubt that. The world needs you.

Say "no" more often. This is hard in our busy world. There is so much need out there, but the world doesn't just need you. It needs a *healthy* version of you. If you're worn out, everyone loses. At the same time, beware of going to the other extreme. I went from always saying yes, to chronically saying no, overly guarding my schedule. We do need to be involved, but we need to make sure what we say "yes" to is right for not just us, but also our family and friends. Here are the criteria I now use:

- Does it support a family member or friend? I will volunteer as a timer at swim meets. I will time at track meets. I will cut cake for the choir concert. I will load drums in a van. I am there to support my family. I will chaperone on the youth mission trip. So the activities that involve my family members always get first dibs on my time. It may sound selfish, but our children are only home with me for a few more years, and I want them to remember me as part of it.

- Does it energize me? There are volunteer efforts I do outside of my family's activities. But, again, my time is so limited, I have to be intentional. If it's something that will refuel me so when I return home I have more of me to give, then "yes," count me in. If not, sorry, maybe ask me again when my kids are out of the home. It's nothing personal, but I guarantee there is someone else out there who will do a much better job than me because it's their passion, and/or they are in a different phase of life.

- Do I want to do it? It may sound harsh, but there are times I'm just plain tired, and I need some down time with Mark or my kids, or my pups. It's okay to sometimes say "no" just because it's "not in you." We are human and there are times we need a break. Which leads us perfectly into the next section...

Rest more. Sometimes we feel drained because we've given all that we've got. There's nothing left in us, and that is okay. We were created to have times of rest. Take periodic walking breaks if life is tense in the office. Lock yourself in a quiet room and breathe if home life is chaotic. Take one day off each week. It doesn't have to be Saturday or Sunday, just take a day off to refuel so you can return to your life a stronger version of you.

Pour back into others. It sounds ironic, but sometimes it's not that we have holes in our buckets draining us. Sometimes we're carrying around too much water in our buckets, and it's wearing us out. Maybe it's time you pour some of that water into the lives of others. Find a younger version of you and be a support to her. Share with her the wisdom you've attained over the years, especially your stories of when you really messed up. Let her know she's not alone. You may appear to have it together now, but you were once "that" mom who went to Target in a bathrobe and went two weeks without a shower. Provide a shoulder for her to cry on, and be quick to give her encouragement. Perhaps it's time to give back and pay it forward.

"MOST OF US HAVE SPENT OUR LIVES BELIEVING MORE THAN WE DO; SPEND THE REST OF IT DOING MORE THAN WE BELIEVE."
—BOB GOFF

Consider This:

- Take a life analysis. Are you fulfilled? Do you go to bed at night excited for the next day, or do you dread it? Is there an area of your life that's draining you? Try to identify it and make the necessary changes needed to plug it.

- What is your gifting? Are you actively working or volunteering in this area? Are you studying, training, preparing, and bettering yourself in this area? Take the necessary steps that will allow you to spend more of your time in your area of giftedness.

CHAPTER 14
THE BUCKET LIST: THINK OUTSIDE OF THE BOX... OR THE BUCKET

> "I DON'T WANT TO GET TO THE END OF MY LIFE AND FIND THAT I LIVED JUST THE LENGTH OF IT. I WANT TO HAVE LIVED THE WIDTH OF IT AS WELL."
> —DIANE ACKERMAN

Mark and I are big dreamers. I don't mean that in a braggadocious way. It's usually silly stuff that we think of while on dates or waiting in the terminal for a flight.

When we were dating, I had a map of the world hanging on my wall. We would spend hours talking on the phone as I looked at that map. We had a dream to take an around-the-world trip. I'd dream of India. He talked of China. I longed for Europe. He was lured to South America. It didn't matter to us. It all sounded incredible, and we both wanted to see it all.

We have yet to do our around-the-world-trip, but in the early part of our marriage, we were able to fulfill some of those dreams. He went to China and Africa with work. We both lived in South America and Europe and took advantage of our time there, visiting many of the surrounding countries. We've also been to Southeast Asia and North Africa. When I look at a map and all the countries we have visited, I feel blessed. We've seen a lot.

But there is still a big hole in my heart.

I have yet to visit India. I'm not sure why India draws me in. It began in college when I was assigned a semester-long project on the culture. Maybe it's because I've made dear friends who are Indian. It could be Bollywood. Perhaps it's the food and the colorful culture. Who knows?

In my 30s, I thought about India all the time. But with the arrival of my babies, I put it on the back burner and forgot about it, until I'd see a movie or a documentary and a small flame would ignite again in my heart. I'd put it out, mainly because of logistical reasons, but it would always return with the next reminder. This is a routine I've repeated numerous times.

India has always been a strong interest for me, but so are other countries. However, I didn't realize how strong of a desire India was for me until I made my Bucket List. Since then, it's a roaring flame in my heart, and I keep praying that one day I will get to experience her beautiful culture and people in person.

> ## "HISTORY WILL BE KIND TO ME, FOR I INTEND TO WRITE IT."
> —WINSTON CHURCHILL

THE POWER OF A BUCKET LIST.

When I began brainstorming the idea of my blog, I thought it would be fun to come up with a Bucket List. Of course, true to my form, I put it off until the last minute. It was the morning of the photo shoot for my website and I was planning out the photos for each section. I needed a photo for my "To Do" section. On a whim, I thought of doing a photo of my Bucket List, so I printed out a sheet and began writing, not fully processing what I put on the list, just whatever popped into my head. Guess what dream was No. 1?

INDIA.

I found it interesting that it was the first thing to pop into my head. Was it just a random thought? Or did it mean something? Could it be that dreams that never die are meant to come true?

Ever since then, I can't get India off of my mind. I see movies with scenes in India, my heart aches. I hear of my friends traveling to India to visit their family, I'm jealous. One time, friends brought me home a souvenir, and I proudly display it in my home. I go to World Market, and I cry. I mean, come on! Talk about an obsession.

There's power in the physical act of writing down goals. It reveals truth. There are other items on that list that don't burn a hole in my soul like India and a few others. The whole exercise revealed to me the importance of writing down your dreams, to the point where I feel I need to share it with you and encourage you to do the same.

You need to make a Bucket List. Not because it's hip. Not because it's cheesy. But because the reflection that is required for the process will search deep in your soul. It will reveal or remind you of desires you had as a child or in your 20s, or 30s, that are seared in your soul, but were covered with either urgent or present circumstances.

TO DO LIST:

1. India
2. Cuba
3. Tour de France
4. Write Book #2
5. Ironman 70.3
6. Lose 10 lbs.
7. Sleep 8 hrs./night
8. date my husband more
9. visit Hawaii
10. start Non-profit
11. do more speaking
12. Dancing With the Stars
13. Dancing with the Stars
14. Spudman Tri
15. Read Bible daily
16. Pray/meditate
17. eat whole foods more
18. Be more organized
19. _____
20. _____
21. _____

Some are possible, others—not so much. For example, I wanted to be a *Solid Gold* dancer in my teens. However, there's no way my body will gyrate like that anymore, much less be willing to go on stage in one of those tiny outfits.

They are still there. Believe me. And, unless you take the time to make your list, they may remain hidden, deep within, only to be remembered when it's too late.

Over time, you'll discover new items to add to your list. Since I made my initial list, I've been reminded of others, and I continue to add and adjust it over time. It's an eternal process. It's helped to keep me dreaming, reminding me to seize each opportunity that comes my way. God continually waves offerings in front of us, but it's up to us to grab them and do our part in making them happen. If you know what it is you want to do, you will then know where to put your focus.

> "MANY PEOPLE DIE WITH THEIR MUSIC STILL IN THEM. WHY IS THIS SO? TOO OFTEN IT IS BECAUSE THEY ARE ALWAYS GETTING READY TO LIVE. BEFORE THEY KNOW IT, TIME RUNS OUT."
> —OLIVER WENDELL HOLMES

KEEP YOUR
LIST NEARBY.

I keep a copy of my Bucket List on my desk and review it periodically. It helps to keep the items on the list fresh in my mind. You would think that if I made the list, I'd remember every item on the list. But we live in a culture full of activity, and it's easy to get distracted. The busyness of life will have us running in circles, and before we know it, we're nowhere close to living out our dreams.

Reviewing my list weekly has helped me stay on course. And, even though I am busy, it's held me accountable to keep working toward certain goals that I normally would have blown off. (And it helps when you post it on the Internet. Talk about accountability!) We've already begun checking some off. Two of which I may have put on hold had they not been on the list.

One of them was traveling to Cuba. Mark and I had talked forever about Cuba. We knew one day the country would be open to Americans again. We just had to be patient. But then, once it did open up, we wanted to see it before it was flooded with Americanism. We wanted to see her true culture.

We were presented with the opportunity of traveling with Fathom Cruise Line on the inaugural trip to Cuba after decades of that travel not being allowed. As the trip got closer, life at home went crazy with the kids' school, with my family, and my mother's surgery, etc. There was a part of me that wondered if we should put off the trip and go at another time, or maybe let Mark and the kids go on this trip and then return with all of us later.

Life's busyness was polluting my mind. Looking back, I can't believe I was even considering staying behind or letting my family go without me. I would be a fool to give up the opportunity of being part of this historical moment.

But that is what a busy life will do to you. It will strangle you, and you make decisions with an oxygen-depleted brain that you end up regretting later. Having a list in front of you fuels you to fight back and take control of your life.

My list kept me accountable. Now I'm sure Mark would have shot me down and not let me stay behind as they went on to Cuba. But the point is, I was seriously considering not going. My list kept me on track. We went and had the time of our lives. Noah and Anastasia experienced history firsthand, and we made memories with friends and other family members. We are still living off of the high from that adventure.

Had I not had my list to encourage me, would I have gone?

"IF YOU DON'T BUILD YOUR DREAM, SOMEONE ELSE WILL HIRE YOU TO BUILD THEIRS."
—TONY GASKINS

WHY DO I NEED A LIST?

We've all been given a limited number of days on Earth. We are not here to do menial tasks, make it through the day, get our job done, eat, sleep, and start again tomorrow. Yes, those jobs need to be done and, by doing them, they provide the means for us to travel, participate in hobbies, care for our families, etc.

Having a list helps your "you" not get lost in the process. Your list doesn't have to be full of international travel. You may have no interest in leaving your hometown. That's okay. Your list should reflect you. Your desires. Your goals. Your dreams.

You may want to make a quilt. You've never done one before, and you don't know where to start. If it's on your list, it will push you to sign up for that class, join that quilting group, or remind you to put aside time each day to work on your quilt. And, before you know it, you'll have a beautiful quilt that *you* made.

Bucket Lists give you hope. Life is hard, and we all have issues in our lives that beat us down. A Bucket List gives you something to dream about that can take you out of the reality of your circumstances. It gives you something to look forward to at the end of the day. Say you want to learn Spanish. You may have a dead-end job that you are stuck with, but at the end of the day, you can go home and work on that Spanish. Your progress excites you and gives you a sense of accomplishment. Before you know it, you've built up the confidence to approach your neighbor, who is a native speaker, and she agrees to let you practice with her. You may even find that you have cultivated a beautiful new friendship, something you never thought you needed before, but realize you now do.

Bucket Lists take you on journeys. They do take effort, but all journeys require you to take that first step. Otherwise, you'll remain stationary, unaware of all that is just beyond your grasp.

"GOALS THAT ARE NOT WRITTEN DOWN ARE JUST WISHES."
—UNKNOWN

STARTING YOUR OWN LIST.

I can't emphasize enough the importance of taking the step to write your own Bucket List. You will not regret it. To make it an easier process, I want to share some guidelines that have helped me.

Bucketstorm. Brainstorm. Spend time with a pad and pen, and write down everything that comes to mind. If it pops up in your mind, write it down. Use no filters during this part of the exercise. Don't limit your thinking. Don't think of logistics or money or age of kids, etc. Just write down the desires of your heart, no matter how big or how small. Think through questions, such as:

- What do you want to see?

- What do you want to experience?

- What goals do you want to achieve?

- What foods do you want to try?

- What cities would you like to visit?

- What musicals would you like to attend?

- What purchases would you like to make?

- What people would you like to meet?

- What mountain would you like to climb (literally and figuratively)?

- What book would you like to read?

Think through relationships. Do you want to marry? Do you want kids? Do you have spiritual goals? A meditation retreat? A fasting retreat?

Let your thoughts flow, and don't hold back. It is during this time you may find your "India."

> ## "WHAT YOU GET BY ACHIEVING YOUR GOALS IS NOT AS IMPORTANT AS WHAT YOU BECOME BY ACHIEVING YOUR GOALS."
> —ZIG ZIGLAR

Don't let the world's present political unrest, terrorism, or any instability affect what you put on your list. The fears you have today may erase the dreams that can become your reality tomorrow. Don't let the uncertainty of today rob you of fulfilling your dream.

Don't have a scarcity mentality when writing your list. Don't think of money or vacation days or kids' school schedules. Those are details you can tackle later. The key here is to have a "the sky's the limit" attitude when bucketstorming. Scarcity thinking will limit you, and if you give up before you try, you'll never see your dreams come to fruition. Remember, anything is possible.

Don't let the negative talk of others influence your list. Aunt Erma may tell you there is no way *you* can learn to cook Asian food. "Honey, you can't cook. You started a fire by boiling water. You saw 'egg whites' in a recipe and you thought it meant *white* eggs. You don't have the cookin' gene in ya!" Don't listen to them. This is *your* life and these are *your* dreams. You can do anything you want if there is a desire. But you won't if you never try. Plus, half the fun of the journey is the mistakes we make along the way. (And, boy, do they make for good stories later!)

CATEGORIZE THE ITEMS ON YOUR LIST.

After you make your initial list (because we all know once we get started, we'll want to add more to the list!), study it, and see if there are natural ways to categorize it. There is no formal or perfect way to do this. Look and see if there is one that matches your present life.

For example, you could organize which ones are most important to you at the top of your list and work your way down to what is least important.

You could arrange them seasonally. In the winter, you can travel to Colorado and learn to ski or make a good pot of soup. With the shorter days, it will be a good time to cuddle up with the book you've always wanted to read. Summertime, the days are longer, you can learn to grill, learn to swim, go to that Caribbean island.

You may be the type who likes to mark things off your list quickly. You can organize it by what is most likely. "I'll be in New Hampshire for work this spring. I can hook it up to a weekend and go see NYC on the same trip." Check.

You can make a "with kids" list and a "post kids" list. Make a list of things to do while your children are still living at home, things you can do as a family. Have another category of items you will do when you're dealing with empty-nest syndrome.

You can keep yourself well rounded and have a travel category, a hobby category, a physical challenge category, emotional health, financial health, and spiritual health categories. This is a good way to keep it from being too top heavy in one area, especially if you are a person who likes balance in life.

The ways to categorize are endless. For some, this step will help focus and organize the best ways to get moving on the list. Others are more free-spirited and like to randomly choose what feels right in the moment. Me, I started my list because I wanted balance in my life. I have a tendency to get hooked on something and go full force with it. I don't want my life to be all about physical challenges or travel. I want to expand my territory and try new things. So having them in categories reveals if I'm neglecting an area of my life.

"A PESSIMIST SEES THE DIFFICULTY IN EVERY OPPORTUNITY; AN OPTIMIST SEES THE OPPORTUNITY IN EVERY DIFFICULTY."
—WINSTON CHURCHILL

SET A
TIMETABLE.

Some items on your list may be time-sensitive, others—not so much. If running in the Chicago Marathon is on your list, it is generally held in October. So you will need to mark that date on your calendar, making sure you have enough time to train for it.

If you want to see cherry blossoms in Washington, D.C., depending on the weather, you usually have a two-week period at the end of March and beginning of April, so you will want to block off a flexible schedule during this time. Then again, with our crazy weather, you could be watching the lighting of the Christmas tree and seeing the cherry blossoms at the same time.

If you want to get a nursing degree, you'll need to apply and begin by a certain time.

Look at what you have on your lists, and see if any of them have deadlines.

For others, there may not be deadlines, but it may be more pleasant if done during a certain season. If your dream is to swim with the polar bears, I wouldn't recommend doing this in the winter. Actually, I wouldn't recommend this one at all. I don't think it has a very high success rate.

"THE QUALITY OF YOUR COMMITMENTS WILL DETERMINE THE COURSE OF YOUR LIFE."
—RALPH MARSTON

GET GOING.

A Bucket List should not be something that makes you anxious. None of us need more items on our "to-do" list that make us feel as if we're not accomplishing much in life. Instead, it should be a mirror that reflects back to you and reveals if you are living the life you want. It can also be a filter through which you make certain choices. "I can buy this designer dress that I will wear only a handful of times. Or I can put this money in my India jar and have memories with my family that will last a lifetime."

You may be like me and have dreams you've held on to for decades. Or there may be dreams that lurk within you, but you aren't even aware they are there.

That is the beauty of a Bucket List, it reveals your heart and then propels you to live.

Start writing. Start planning. Start living.

"AND IN THE END, IT'S NOT THE YEARS IN YOUR LIFE THAT COUNT. IT'S THE LIFE IN YOUR YEARS."
—ABRAHAM LINCOLN

NEED SOME HELP GETTING STARTED?

Sometimes our brainstorming efforts need a little jump-start. Below is a list of random categories and items that can be added to any list. One trick I read about was to first think locally and then think globally. Warm up with what is around you and then your brain will be open to reaching for the stars.

Family—Do you want to start a family? (Or get the kids to finally move out?) Do you want to adopt or foster a child? Do you want to move into a new home? Do you want more playtime with your kids?

Education—Are there degrees, certificates, or training you would like to earn that would enhance your life and career?

Vacations—Are there family getaways, couple retreats? Disney? Caribbean? Florida? California? Maine? Europe? Africa? Australia?

Vocation—Are there work-related dreams? Do you imagine starting your own company? Working for a non-profit? Earning top salesman of the year?

Hobbies—What hobbies have you longed to try? Culinary, acting, singing, knitting, painting, calligraphy, running, swimming, cello, skiing, reading, fishing, hunting, golf, crafts, drums, dancing, woodworking, Sumo wrestling? (Hey, don't judge. We gotta be open minded—let it flow!)

Shows—Are there musicals you want to see? (Hello... Hamilton!) Symphonies? Operas? Choirs?

Cities—Are there cities you've wanted to visit? Chicago? Atlanta? Portland? Paris? Munich? New York? Paducah? (I didn't say anything about size!)

Different forms of travel—Do you want to travel cross-country in a train? Fly in a private jet? Sail around the world? Bike across Canada? Take a rocket into space?

Do you want to be a streaker?—Did that get your attention? I'm not talking about any nakedness. I mean hold a streak (e.g., run every day for a year). Swim every day for a week (my kind of streak!). Journal every day. Begin each day with yoga for as many days as possible.

Physical goals—Lose 20, 30, 100 pounds? Run a 5K race? Run a marathon in all 50 states? Become a yogi? Build your strength?

Mentor—Do you want to give back? Mentor a young mother? Volunteer in a school? Help prisoners earn their GED? Coach a softball team?

Volunteer—Work with refugees? Feed the homeless? Do relief work? Build wells in Africa? Teach English as a second language? Hang bulletin boards in your kids' schools?

This doesn't even touch the tip of the iceberg. The possibilities are endless. The important thing is anything you put on your list needs to breathe life into you. If it scares you, start small and work your way up. Before you know it, you will awaken the big dreams that have been lying dormant deep within your heart.

Perhaps the No. 1 item on all of our Bucket Lists is to actually do the things on our Bucket List. Let's get living!

"IF YOU WANT YOUR LIFE TO BE A MAGNIFICENT STORY,
THEN BEGIN BY REALIZING THAT YOU ARE THE AUTHOR,
AND EVERY DAY YOU HAVE THE OPPORTUNITY TO WRITE A
NEW PAGE."
—MARK HOULAHAN

Consider This:

- Do you have a Bucket List? Set aside some time, first by yourself, and then with your partner, and make a list of your dreams. Prioritize or categorize them as you see fit, and go for it. Start living the life you've always dreamed of but were afraid to try.

- Make a Bucket List.

- Mark a Bucket List.

ONWARD: WE'VE ONLY JUST BEGUN

> "TRANSFORMATION IS A PROCESS, AND AS LIFE HAPPENS THERE ARE TONS OF UPS AND DOWNS. IT'S A JOURNEY OF DISCOVERY—THERE ARE MOMENTS ON MOUNTAINTOPS AND MOMENTS IN DEEP VALLEYS OF DESPAIR."
> —RICK WARREN

Years ago, when Mark and I decided we wanted to do a triathlon, we joined our local YMCA. They have a triathlon club with coaches who would guide and coach us along our journey. When we started, Mark and I knew how to swim, but we were so inefficient that we could only swim one length and would then hold on to the side of the wall, gasping for air, coughing up water, and then would return to the other side of the pool, only to do it all over again. Unfortunately, I'm not exaggerating...at all.

We both had ridden bikes since we were kids and had run numerous road races (although, in my case, the word "run" is to be taken very lightly). So we mainly focused on the swimming. It wasn't until the weather warmed up and

I was able to ride my bike outside that I realized I needed help on the bike as well.

It took a while for the bike and me to become friends. (What an understatement!)

My first bike "incident" was at a crosswalk on a busy street. Cars on both sides of the road stopped and waited to let me cross. I mounted my bike and started to pedal. The cleat on the bottom of my biking shoe slipped. I wobbled and coasted toward a hole. I tried to miss, but somehow hit it straight on, lost my balance, and slammed down on my left side. Some of the drivers pretended not to see me while others couldn't hide behind their obvious smirks. Humiliated, I unclipped my other cleat and ran across the street, pushing my bike. I cowered behind some trees until they all passed (praying no one I knew was in that car line).

Another time I was on an easy ride on our local greenbelt. I approached a runner heading in the same direction as me. I announced my presence and was about to pass her on the left when I noticed a groove in the middle of the pavement. I tried to avoid it, but somehow my front tire made its way directly inside the groove. Luckily, I didn't go over my handlebars, but I again began to wobble and couldn't unclick the cleat on my shoe fast enough. I toppled over again in front of my runner friend, whose facial expressions volleyed between concern and amusement.

Unfortunately, I have many more of these stories, and one day was sharing my frustration (and pain) with one of the coaches, "I don't understand. I've ridden a bike since I was three. I shouldn't be falling this much. How come every time I see an obstacle in my path, I hit it head on?"

He went on to explain to me that my problem was that I was focusing on the objects blocking my path instead of where I wanted to go. "Your body and bike will follow where your eyes go. You have to focus on your path, not the obstacle."

Wow! This was huge. Not only did it help my biking, but it gave me a new principle in life. How many times have we set out on our journeys only to have them blocked by obstacles in our path? Instead of floating around them, we hit them head on and then flee to the side of the road. So many times in my life I've gotten stuck because I'm too focused on what is blocking my path instead of the clearing that is to the right or left.

Our lives will follow what we focus on. If we spend all our time focusing on our difficulties, our limitations, we won't move forward. We only need to see them enough to know to avoid them and then immediately need to work to find our new passage.

There is so much greatness within you. I'd hate for the world to miss out seeing it because a hitch in the road has sidelined you.

There's a well-known story in the Bible (Matthew 14:22-33) where Jesus sent His disciples out on a boat to cross the water as He stayed behind to say His goodbyes to the crowds and to have some alone time to pray. It took awhile, and night fell as Jesus prayed.

During this time, Jesus' disciples were alone in the boat in strong winds, fighting the waves. Around 3:00 a.m., they see in the distance Jesus walking *on* the water. At first they freaked out, believing Him to be a ghost. It doesn't say this in the text, but I'm pretty sure it was the first time any of them had seen someone walk on water.

Jesus called out to them, telling them to chill, not to worry, that it was Him. His disciple, Peter, tested Him saying in so many words, "If it's really you, then call me out there, and let me walk on water, too!"

He did, and Peter stepped out of the boat and began to walk toward Jesus, *on* the water. But the winds were still blowing. Peter panicked the moment he took his eyes off Jesus to focus instead on the waves. He immediately began to sink.

Whether you are a person of faith or not, there is a great life principle in this story. Do you want to live a life watching others do the impossible and great things with their lives? Or do you want to step out of that boat and feel the thrill of doing what most felt was impossible?

Remember, there is the opportunity for all of us to live out our dreams. It's not an either her or you. That is the myth of scarcity talking. Just because another girlfriend is living her dream (or your dream), doesn't mean there is not enough room for you as well. If she's a gifted speaker and you want to be a speaker, too, go for it. It's not either/ or. You both have something to give the world that only *you* can fulfill.

I've always wondered what it was like for the other disciples in the boat, watching Peter walk on water. Did they wonder if they could have walked on water as well if they had the faith to try? Were they numb by fear? Did the present circumstances of the storm trick them into believing it was safer, more practical, to stay in the boat? What would have happened if they, too, had asked Jesus to call them out of the boat? We will never know, but if you ask me, we would have read about 12 men experiencing the impossible, instead of just one. And maybe, if all his friends were out there with him, Peter may have had more confidence and wouldn't have sunk.

It's not too late for you. It's not too late for me. We can't use age or time as an excuse anymore. If we focus, muster the courage to step out of the boat, we can experience the impossible at any age. If we do it together, we can encourage one another along the way. We can pull each other up when we fall and we can celebrate together in our victories.

God didn't create us to live our lives inside the boat. He created us to walk on the water with Him. If we're still breathing, we still have the opportunity to step out of that boat. We just have to focus and believe. *Believe,* my friend. It's inside of you and the world needs what you have to give. It's time we quit hiding in the trees. Let's step out and live!

"THE WAY TO GET STARTED IS TO QUIT TALKING AND BEGIN DOING."
—WALT DISNEY

"EACH DAY IS A NEW DAY, A NEW OPPORTUNITY TO WORK TOWARD MAKING YOUR LIFE THE WAY YOU WANT IT."
—JOSIE CLUNEY

LET'S KEEP IN TOUCH!

My journey may have begun due to me turning 50, but transformation is a life-long journey. I'd love to stay in touch with you. If you'd like to continue reading more of my journey, and share yours with me, check out my blog, **journeyto50.org**. You can also follow me on Facebook at **Laurie Deaton Russell.**

I've so enjoyed my time with you and pray it has been a blessing for you as well!

AUTHOR BIO

Laurie Russell is co-founder of Elevate Publishing. She is a speaker and writes weekly on her blog, Journeyto50.org. She has lived and worked in Russia, Chile, and Germany and currently lives in Boise, Idaho with her husband Mark, their children, Noah and Anastasia, and a random and growing assortment of pets.

elevate
publishing

**DELIVERING TRANSFORMATIVE MESSAGES
TO THE WORLD**

Visit www.elevatepub.com for our latest offerings.

NO TREES WERE HARMED IN THE MAKING OF THIS BOOK.

OK, so a few did make the ultimate sacrifice.

In order to steward our environment, we are partnered with *Plant With Purpose*, to plant a tree for every tree that paid the price for the printing of this book.

To learn more, visit www.elevatepub.com/about

PLANT W TH PURPOSE | WWW.PLANTWITHPURPOSE.ORG